RENEWAL

Sophie Cousins is an award-winning journalist and writer. After almost a decade of working and living overseas, she returned temporarily to Australia to report on the COVID-19 pandemic and its aftermath. Her work has been published in the *Guardian*, *New York Times*, *Foreign Policy*, *London Review of Books* and *Atlantic*, among many others. She has received numerous grants and fellowships including from the National Geographic Society, the International Reporting Project and the South Asian Journalists Association. Her first book, *A Woman's Worth*, was published in 2019.

sophiecousins.com
@SophCousins

SOPHIE COUSINS

NEW REAL

FIVE PATHS TO A FAIRER AUSTRALIA

TEXT PUBLISHING MELBOURNE AUSTRALIA

textpublishing.com.au

The Text Publishing Company
Swann House, 22 William Street, Melbourne, Victoria 3000, Australia

Published by The Text Publishing Company, 2021

Cover design by Chong W.H.
Page design by Rachel Aitken
Typeset by J&M Typesetting

Printed and bound in Australia by Griffin Press, an accredited ISO/NZS 1401:2004 Environmental Management System printer

ISBN: 9781922330901 (paperback)
ISBN: 9781922459046 (ebook)

A catalogue record for this book is available from the National Library of Australia

This book is printed on paper certified against the Forest Stewardship Council® Standards. Griffin Press holds FSC chain-of-custody certification SGS-COC-005088. FSC promotes environmentally responsible, socially beneficial and economically viable management of the world's forests.

To my mum, who taught me to always find the light amid the dark

CONTENTS

INTRODUCTION

'The risk to the Australian public from this novel virus remains relatively low.'

CHIEF MEDICAL OFFICER PROFESSOR BRENDAN MURPHY, 21 JANUARY 2020

'There is a way through this. We all need to keep going. I need all of you to keep going.'

PRIME MINISTER SCOTT MORRISON, 20 MARCH 2020

It would be disconcerting to wake up one day and discover that everything in our inner and outer sanctum had fundamentally changed; that all that we thought was real and safe in the world, in our world, was no longer.

Did you wake up one morning and realise that the world as you knew it had changed beyond recognition? Or was it a more gradual process in which normality was gradually stripped away, restriction by restriction, until there was nowhere left to go?

I was on holiday in Ecuador in January 2020, knee-deep in snow, clutching my ice axe and climbing mountains, disconnected from my urban life and immersed in my preferred reality. It was only when I travelled back to my home in Kathmandu in February that I began to re-engage with the news and truly understand that this new and deadly virus circulating may be more than a flu in the far-away city of Wuhan—which in reality was actually not that far from Nepal.

Arriving at Kathmandu's International Airport to immigration officers and health officials wearing masks and temperature-checking passengers was an awakening. At the time just one case of COVID-19 had been confirmed in the Himalayan nation. Nepal felt safe.

It wasn't until early March, however, that I began to grasp the magnitude of the novel coronavirus and the impact it could have, not just on loved ones far away in Australia, but on the world as we knew it.

My mum called me from Sydney on 12 March, the day after the World Health Organization (WHO) declared COVID-19 a pandemic and two weeks after Prime Minister Scott Morrison had announced the virus would become a pandemic. She was calling to tell me that the barista at her local coffee shop, where she gets her weak skim-milk cappuccino every morning after walking the dog, had tested positive for COVID-19.

That was the moment in which the pandemic was no longer an abstract problem. That was my moment when the pandemic became real.

I felt my stomach twist and churn with anxiety, caffeine running through my veins. 'Please do not go anywhere near that coffee shop,' I pleaded. 'In fact, Mum, please just don't go out. This is serious.'

I knew I was being alarmist, but with our limited understanding of the virus at the time, extreme caution was all I had.

By 12 March 2020, the coronavirus had been in Australia for forty-seven days. Infections stood at 142 confirmed cases. A few days later, the Department of Foreign Affairs and Trade issued advice recommending Australians abroad who wished to return home do so as soon as possible via commercial flights. Tens of thousands of Australians who live and work overseas were forced to think about the concept of home. Is home defined by people or place, or both? The concept takes on a new meaning during a pandemic. Where is 'home' when the world turns dark?

By mid to late March, life as we knew it had drastically changed in Australia. Gripped by fear, people emptied supermarket shelves. Hand sanitiser. Canned food. Flour. Rice. Sugar. All gone. But it was toilet paper that was our undoing. Perhaps buying utilitarian items gave us a sense of control over a situation that was out of control. Perhaps it was indicative of our lack of faith in government, faith that had been so damaged by the response to the previous summer's devastating bushfires.

The concept of physical distancing—or rather, our initial lack of respect for it—made international headlines on 20 March, when thousands descended on Bondi Beach for a swim. The previous day, 2700 passengers had disembarked the cruise ship *Ruby Princess* in Sydney, which would not only lead to a national tragedy but signal a reprehensible failure on the part of the NSW Department of Health.

By Monday 23 March, pubs, clubs, cafes and restaurants were shut, along with gyms, indoor sporting venues, cinemas, nightclubs and casinos. A few days later, states began shutting their borders, the first time since the Spanish flu pandemic a century earlier. International travel was also banned. Our globalised world reverted to its smallest constituent parts.

Australia's total case tally topped three thousand on 27 March, doubling in just three days. By Sunday 29 March, we were in full lockdown and only allowed out of our homes for one of a few essential reasons.

People over the age of seventy were advised to self-isolate, as were people over the age of sixty with chronic diseases or comorbidities. All Aboriginal and Torres Strait Islander peoples over the age of fifty with chronic diseases were asked to stay home, exposing our appalling inability to improve the health of our Indigenous peoples.

Australian life as we knew it changed beyond recognition. Time became irrelevant. Is it Sunday or Thursday? Does it even matter? What does?

'I should say at the outset that we are not Italy, we are not the United States, we are not Spain,' Professor Brendan Murphy, the then chief medical officer, told the nation at the end of March.

As the weeks unfolded, Australia also revealed itself to not be the United Kingdom, France, Brazil, Russia and almost every country on the planet facing the pandemic, with a few exceptions, such as Taiwan, New Zealand, Thailand, Sri Lanka and Vietnam. It in fact revealed itself to be a model of how to effectively respond to this new and deadly virus.

While we had the advantage of time and geography, it was so much more than that. Forming a National Cabinet of federal and state leaders—akin to a war cabinet—to guide a unified, inclusive response, Australia chose to put politics aside and place medical experts at the centre of the response. State and territory premiers and chief ministers from both the left and the right worked together to plot the course of the nation through the crisis. In stark contrast to the issue of climate change, we chose science over ideology, and evidence-based policy over opinion-based policy.

Scott Morrison gave up on delivering a budget surplus and instead committed $320 billion to support households and businesses through the economic blows of the pandemic (though it was later revealed there was a $60 billion reporting error in the cost of JobKeeper). Unemployment benefits doubled, a wage subsidy program was introduced—though it was not universal—and child care was made free, albeit temporarily.

Queues of people waiting to access Centrelink payments filled our television screens. They served as a critical reminder that any one of us can fall through the cracks.

With the government abandoning its parameters on fiscal restraint, so much of what we believed to be true collapsed. We could afford to raise the Newstart Allowance and we could afford to provide free child care. Had such economic measures been introduced months earlier, they would have been branded as 'dangerous socialism' by Morrison's party, wrote novelist Richard Flanagan in the *New York Times*.

As devastating images of overflowing morgues from New York City to Rome also filled our television screens, it soon felt like we were facing an entirely different virus to the rest of the world. But that feeling was premature. The virus proved us wrong.

A bungled hotel quarantine program in Victoria led to Australia's second—and far more devastating—wave. Melbourne was locked down for an additional four months, with other parts of Victoria restricted too. We watched from the confines of our homes as the rest of the country was open for business. It felt unfair and unjust.

But if we needed anything more heartbreaking than the social isolation, job losses and countless businesses collapsing, it was what unfolded in residential aged care. The coronavirus swept through vulnerable homes with precarious casual staff members, taking victims at every corner. At the time of writing, three-quarters of deaths from COVID-19 in Australia have been in private aged-care homes. These are deaths that could have been prevented. They will remain a blight on this nation for decades to come.

While the prolonged lockdown in Victoria was hard, it was necessary. Thousands of deaths were prevented. We do not need to look far to see what could have been. At the time of writing, Europe is in the midst of its second deadly wave. Cases in the United States are at an all-time high.

If combating COVID-19 is considered an invisible war, then Australia can be proud of why we got into the fight: to preserve life. Our response to the pandemic—one that was based on inclusion, fairness, resilience and communality—brought home the fact that we are more united than ever. It has illustrated that change is possible; there is hope for the future.

Perhaps the biggest lesson we've learnt from COVID-19 is that there are alternatives—it is possible to pursue a different path.

This is a time of reawakening and of re-engagement. We are realising that the truths we understood as immutable, the basis of our social order, are actually not rigid and inevitable, but constructions of our own making. We can reshape them.

In the face of this crisis, we have been afforded a great privilege: the chance to reassess the principles and values that underpin our society, and rebuild accordingly. We now must ensure that the same values that have guided our fight against COVID-19 endure and expand into other aspects of society. How can we use this critical juncture to create a better, more just Australia? What would a fair and equal, green and healthy, secure and smarter Australia look like? What would it take to get there?

As an Australian who unexpectedly temporarily returned 'home' after almost a decade living and working overseas, I've grappled with some fundamental questions in writing this book. It's forced me to think about the values I stand for, and the type of country I want to be proud to belong to.

Incorporating interviews with some of our best, brightest and most progressive thinkers alongside the voices of ordinary Australians, this book splits into five major areas of discussion: government and politics; welfare; Indigenous affairs; health and education; and climate change and industry. Taking COVID-19 as the starting point, each chapter will set out what the progressive ideal looks like in Australia, and how we could bring this ideal about.

Underlying each chapter is also a critique of neoliberalism, a term that has become ubiquitous in mainstream media and international institutions. It is an ideology that has come to dominate our thoughts, beliefs, culture and politics. It is critical to understand what the term means in order to make sense of where we are right now, how we got here and where we need to go.

I like the Canadian academic Kean Birch's simple definition best: neoliberalism is 'used to refer to an economic system in which the "free" market is extended to every part of our public and personal worlds'. He goes on to write, in the *Conversation*, that 'the transformation of the state from a provider of public welfare to a promoter of markets and competition helps to enable this shift'. Echoing this definition,

Richard Denniss, chief economist at the Australia Institute, argues that neoliberalism can be understood as an 'ideology focused on the idea that market forces are superior to government decision-making'.

The term was coined back in 1938 but it wasn't until the 1970s and the ascent of politicians like Margaret Thatcher and Ronald Reagan that neoliberal ideas began to enter the mainstream. Massive tax cuts for the rich, privatisation and deregulation, among other policies, made sweeping changes to how societies and economies function. As Thatcher famously declared in the 1980s, 'There's no such thing as a society. There are individual men and women and there are families.'

In Australia, embracing neoliberalism has meant that we have sold off public assets and privatised institutions that were once public. It has led us to believe that we are consumers, rather than citizens, in a world where competition is the bedrock of human relationships.

Neoliberalism aside, regrettably but also inevitably this book cannot cover every pressing topic in contemporary Australian society. I would love to have covered critical issues surrounding asylum seekers and refugees, agriculture, rural and remote affairs, gender and women's rights, and community services. But given the parameters of the book, I had to choose the most immediate areas for discussion.

As I write this, the world is searching for a vaccine for this deadly virus. We know that if a vaccine does become available, Australia will not price people out; it will be available for all. In that sense, a vaccine is a panacea for a country like ours. But it will not bring back the world as we knew it. That world is long gone.

As our relationship with nature continues to deteriorate, there will be many more crises that we will have to overcome. There will be no vaccine for megafires or droughts or rising sea levels. Nor will there be a vaccine for the next pandemic. We cannot inoculate ourselves against increasing inequality, or political and social marginalisation, or the devastating treatment of our Indigenous peoples.

Perhaps the cure for our crises—those we face right now and the ones we cannot yet imagine—is right here in front of us, and always has been: to work together for the common good.

1 | GOVERNMENT AND POLITICS

> 'There are no blue teams or red teams. There are no more unions or bosses. There are just Australians now; that's all that matters.'
>
> PRIME MINISTER SCOTT MORRISON, 2 APRIL 2020

Prior to the COVID-19 pandemic and the devastating bushfires of 2019–20, it would have been reasonable to believe that Australia was a nation divided. That was what the media had been telling us, and that's what the politics illustrated. Apparently, we didn't agree on much.

Fear had inevitably grown, and so had mistrust. Not just trust in government and our politicians—which had significantly declined—but trust in each other, too.

Polls signalled it. The latest World Values Survey 2017–20 recorded that social trust in Australia—trust between people—was at an all-time low of 49 per cent in 2019.

For a country like Australia, where we pride ourselves on the notion of mateship, the idea that we are increasingly wary of each other is, for lack of a better word, sad. Are we really fearful of our neighbours and of strangers on the street? Are we really that disconnected, really in such broad disagreement on issues from climate change to public housing?

If we're told for so long to be wary of our neighbours with overgrown beards, to be fearful of 'boat people' who want to steal our insecure jobs, and to shame those on welfare because they are wasting taxpayers' dollars, then it is no surprise that we are less trusting of one another. We live in a society that has sold off almost everything we own in common, from public parks to education. The gulf between rich and poor has deepened, and immigrant communities continue to face social and political marginalisation. Is it any wonder that Australians feel left behind and disconnected, less trusting of one another and of the institutions and systems that govern our lives?

After years of tumultuous politics and the sight of politicians serving themselves and their mates before than the public interest, it is no surprise that Australians have become increasingly disillusioned with their political class. This has become evident not only in polls indicating declining trust in politicians and government, but in voting behaviour. The Grattan Institute's 2018 report 'A Crisis of Trust' found that the share of votes for minor parties and independents had skyrocketed since 2007. At the 2016 election it reached its highest level since the Second World War and that trend continued into the 2019 election. 'The minor party vote is mostly a protest vote against the major parties: a vote for "anyone but them"...Falling trust in government explains much of the dissatisfaction,' the report says.

Richard Denniss, chief economist at the Australia Institute, writes in his 2018 Quarterly Essay, *Dead Right*, that 'it is easier to control a community when it is fearful and divided than when it is confident and united'. 'Australian governments no longer seek to reassure those living in fear,' he writes. 'Neoliberalism has taught us that such fear is valuable.'

But such fear is destructive; it changes the way we see ourselves and others, and fundamentally alters the society in which we live.

In a time of crisis, though, we have shown that we are not fearful and divided. We realise that we are better together than apart. The blossoming of mutual aid—voluntary cooperation for a common purpose—first in the bushfires and then during the COVID-19 pandemic, has showed us that we are cohesive; that our notion of mateship, of helping one another out, is very much alive and well, despite evidence to the contrary.

On 30 December 2019, Manpreet Singh and his small army of volunteers made their way towards the East Gippsland region of Victoria with a food van loaded with groceries and cooking equipment. They set up camp at the relief centre at Bairnsdale City Oval, opened up their van and began serving hot meals to the hundreds of people who had been forced to evacuate due to the bushfires, along with the police, firefighters, army and other emergency personnel. Plumes of smoke rose kilometres into the sky behind them.

What the volunteers, from Melbourne-based non-profit Sikh Volunteers Australia, thought would be a two- or three-day trip ended up being sixteen continuous days. The group woke at 4 a.m. every day to prepare food that they would serve late into the evening as the smell of smoke and ash lingered in the air.

'When we arrived that first night, we saw that people really needed food,' says Manpreet, who came to Australia in 2005 to study hospitality and who has since gone on to help the homeless and disabled.

'We realised that people really needed our help. The bushfires were only five kilometres away.'

When I speak to Manpreet at the end of May 2020, a few months into the pandemic, he and his volunteers have been running a home delivery meals service for the previous seventy days, with donations from the community.

By April, at the height of the first lockdown, the group was delivering eight hundred hot meals a day across fifteen of Melbourne's suburbs. They served single mums, the elderly, those who had lost their jobs and international students.

'When we serve food, we always talk to people, we know their pain. This is the time where people need our help,' Manpreet says. 'When you help someone, it gives you energy.'

Manpreet's story is remarkable, but it is no anomaly. His is just one of countless stories of people coming together to help one another in times of need.

Tim Hollo is the executive director of the Green Institute, where he leads thinking around ecological political philosophy and practice. For him, the flowering of mutual aid during the bushfires, quickly followed by the pandemic, created space for trust in each other and trust in our communities. 'In the bushfires, governments basically vacated the field and people went, "Well, we're just going to do stuff," and so people started coming together in cooking co-ops and distributing food to people in need and opening their spare rooms to those who'd lost their homes and making gloves and booties for burnt koalas,' he says. 'People came together and did the things that they saw needed to be done because they knew government wasn't going to do it.'

When the pandemic arrived, mutual aid flourished on a much

larger scale. People began knocking on doors to let their neighbours know they could collect groceries or medicines, while online support groups proliferated and supplies in food banks swelled. People opened up their empty homes to enable people to self-isolate, while community centres became refuges for the homeless, or for women and children escaping domestic violence. People brimmed with innovative ideas for how we could remain connected as we became increasingly physically distanced. Rarely had we been closer. It signalled our desire for human connection and cooperation—the very things that have enabled civilisation to thrive. We confirmed we were not mere individuals in a global free market, but that our lives are interconnected, interdependent and intertwined.

'I think some of what we're seeing reflects the demise of traditional institutions who've brought that on themselves,' political scientist and professor at Griffith University Anne Tiernan says. 'I think the kind of things we will see are very localised and that localism was built into the federal design because you had to accommodate diversity and difference. That's why, to me at least, that's still a valid way of organising.'

During the early days of the pandemic, I visited Wilcannia, a remote, predominantly Aboriginal community in far western NSW. There I spent time with a group of women who were running a meals-on-wheels service for the elderly and vulnerable, and with families who had set up camp by the Darling River to give their overcrowded homes, which were brimming with relatives, space to breathe.

I met Monica Kerwin, the Barkindji woman running the meals-on-wheels service, which delivered three hot meals a week to members of the community. Twice a week Monica would make the four-hundred-kilometre round journey to the nearest town of

Broken Hill to purchase trolleys full of produce. 'If you have a lot of people under one roof because of our overcrowding problem, we can take the burden off by cooking an additional meal,' she says. 'It also takes the economic pressure off a bit—there are affordability issues here.'

In between volunteering and taking care of her sick husband, Monica also played a critical role in educating people about COVID-19 and in advocating for strict measures to be implemented to help protect the vulnerable community.

Like Manpreet's, Monica's story of dedication and connection to her community is inspiring. But again, it's not an exception. Seldom have more people's lives been threatened and more people (who have also been affected) put themselves forward to help out. The outpouring of effort in helping others during the pandemic was striking.

As some people went inwards, others went outwards. Some people did both. Something inside all of us shifted as we lived through a shared experience like no other before. It didn't just deepen the bond between us; it sharpened our opinion of our place in the world, with nature.

'If at the heart of our problems for a long time has been this paradigm of disconnection, what the pandemic has shown is that that has always been nonsense; that there is nothing but connection,' Hollo says. 'We are all about connection. Ecologists teach us that an individual part of an ecology is only as healthy as every other part of the ecology...The pandemic has pushed right into our minds to understand that all of us are only as healthy as everybody else is healthy, and that we're only as safe as everybody is well-behaved and looking out for each other. I think this massively changes the way we view the world.'

When the Australian government essentially shut down the country and introduced a nationwide lockdown, it was following its public-policy tradition of insulating the community from exogenous shocks. 'It tells you something about the resilience of Australia's public-policy tradition that our community won't tolerate governments not doing anything...I love the fact that it is still there despite the numerous efforts to fragment it. That's deep, deep, deep, deep in the collective,' Tiernan says.

But it's critical to remember that we were the ones who supported one another through mutual aid or by simply picking up the phone and calling our neighbours, friends and family, near and far, to say, 'Hello, I'm here for you.' We showed one another that we would do everything in our power to protect the lives of our fellow Aussies, new and old.

As we cultivated new ways of connecting and supporting one another, exercising our agency in new and exciting ways, the police roamed the streets enforcing COVID-19 health orders, looking for people to fine. White women breastfeeding alone on park benches became targets and so did white parents teaching their children how to drive. Well, at least that was what we were led to believe by our television screens. Close scrutiny by the *Saturday Paper* of fines in NSW, though—the only state that released detailed information about people fined under the orders—found a disproportionate number were issued in areas largely populated by Indigenous or immigrant Australians. Sadly, this didn't come as a shock. We were then told that downloading the COVIDSafe app to facilitate seamless contact tracing was the 'ticket to ensuring that we can have eased restrictions'—like sunscreen to protect Australians from the virus—before it soon became effectively irrelevant.

As the virus became a showdown between state governments and the federal government, one could ponder whether the latter's swift, decisive and sometimes polarising approach to the pandemic was partially driven by its failure to act following the bushfires.

For a country like Australia, which has a relatively successful democracy, 'it's quite difficult for us to look at those who hold power and see that, more than anything else, they want to hold onto power', Hollo says. 'When ideas of ways of sharing that power start to flourish, distributing that power more equitably around the country, and people taking power back for themselves and exercising it collectively and collaboratively, it's an extraordinary threat.'

The challenge now is how we can mobilise around the shift in consciousness that the pandemic has generated. How can we harness this trust, this connectedness, this engagement in our communities to create a better Australia? How can we repurpose the infrastructure that perpetuates power to remain where it is to support this newly harnessed alternative? How can we cultivate this widely distributed, collective power that serves the people rather than the select few?

POWER TO THE PEOPLE

Power is a dirty word. It conjures up images of corruption, toxicity, greed, middle-aged white men. It doesn't have to, though, if we reshape our understanding of what power is, and ultimately reshape power itself.

The French historian and philosopher Michel Foucault asks us to understand that 'power is not a thing'. It's not the accumulation of wealth or goods, nor is it hierarchical and transactional. Power is everywhere you look; it's negotiated through the different types of relationships people have with one another. Power is complex; it operates at multiple levels, interweaving and intersecting like a spider building its cobweb.

On the surface, this makes sense. We know that power is not just confined to those who walk the corridors of Parliament House. But deeper down, it's difficult for us to grasp that fundamental truth. Maybe we struggle because of growing inequality, the gradual but tangible decline in people power, our disenchantment with a political elite who don't listen, and the widespread belief that competition is the only way to decipher who and what is valuable. But it's a truth we must understand to take control of the reins of power.

Linguist Chi Luu argues in her essay 'Towards a Reconception of Power' that:

> The evolving customs of our communities have grown crueller and more punitive, and our futures have grown bleaker as the needs of the people clash against the desires of that impersonal, immovable force that we obliquely call 'the powers that be'. Entrenched in the very language we use, these are powers that just are, and seemingly always have been, in our governments, big corporations, the elite classes or anyone else to whom we've given power over our lives.

People power is exercised when large numbers of the population express—or act upon—their opinions in a nonviolent manner, to place pressure on the political elite, businesses and other powerful institutions. It is the ability to crave and demand change, and feel that it is possible. The loss of people power in Australia—and not just here—is palpable. This loss doesn't just refer to the physical stripping away of power, though that has very much been happening. We can find evidence of it in the targeting of whistleblowers and the media who report favourably on them, or the NSW Supreme Court order that ruled Sydney's Black Lives Matter protest was unlawful under COVID-19 restrictions (a ruling that was overturned at the last minute).

The loss of people power is also the loss of faith and trust in government and democracy. With that comes a loss of faith in change for the better, and a loss of faith in fighting a battle that feels hopeless. 'It doesn't matter. Nothing will change. Nothing ever changes. Why bother. No one cares. It's pointless.' Sound familiar? That attitude represents a loss in people power. Such rhetoric has become engrained in the way many of us speak about the things we care and worry about—from the cost of university education to our inhumane treatment of asylum seekers and refugees. Can you really blame us?

When people are pushed out of democratic engagement and their faith in the role of government is undermined, people power is reduced to buying things we don't need and action on the individual level.

Perpetuating this loss is the language of neoliberalism, which tells us that competition—not just in the market, but among ourselves—is the bedrock of society and the economy. It tells us we are nobodies unless we are efficient, productive and competitive players. And it has convinced us that the best way forward is to transfer economic control from the public sector to the private sector, which is ostensibly more efficacious. But our individual pursuit of economic growth has come at a cost.

As Richard Denniss writes in *Dead Right*:

> While the policy agenda of neoliberalism has never been broadly applied in Australia, for thirty years the

> language of neoliberalism has been applied to everything from environmental protection to care of the disabled. The result of the partial application of policy and the broad application of language is not just a yawning gap between those with the greatest wealth and those with the greatest need, but a country that is now riven by demographic, geographic and racial divides.

The power of neoliberal language is that it influences our social realities to the extent that it becomes so engrained in our daily reality that we neither notice it nor question it. As Chi Luu suggests, it might mean that we hold certain beliefs (those on the dole are dole bludgers), act in certain ways (I can't afford to take a day off because I must save to buy a house) or support ideologies counter to our values (only those with private health insurance should be afforded the highest level of care).

Much of neoliberalism's rhetorical power comes from the assumption that 'there is no alternative', as Richard Denniss says. This, of course, is bullshit. The world is full of alternatives. The government showed us that even alternatives that we never thought possible are possible when it abolished its neoliberal strictures on fiscal restraint during the pandemic.

Institutional and cultural power structures may have got us to where we are now, but the pandemic and its aftermath have provided us with a tremendous opportunity to realign them and disperse power among ourselves. What if we started by resetting the way we speak? But more than that, what if we reconceptualised power and wielded our own to make changes rather than waiting for them to happen? What if we brought about a form of power that is consistent with our values?

Luu argues that our 'well-worn, conventional language about power makes us less aware of how to achieve a sustainable balance of power, where everybody must play a role.' There is urgent need for us to recognise that, as a nation with arguably the most successful democracy and that is home to the most ancient civilisation on Earth, we share a collective responsibility to come together to work for a better Australia for all of us.

'Despair is not an option, otherwise the forces of bad will win,' says political scientist and professor at Griffith University Anne Tiernan.

•••

'I have always maintained that wherever there are women's and children's interests to be considered, women should be there to consider them,' Vida Goldstein, a young woman from Melbourne who was Australia and New Zealand's sole delegate to the International Women Suffrage Conference, told an audience in 1902 in Washington DC.

In 1902, the newly federated nation of Australia became the only country where white women could both vote and stand for election on an equal basis with white men. It was this coincidence of voting and representation rights that made Australian women the most emancipated in the world. But they didn't get there by chance. It was the result of determined, collaborative activism led by a group of women who imagined what Australia could be like and fought for it.

Suffragists from Brisbane to Perth went beyond advocacy and mobilisation: they organised. They engendered public support for their demands by creating solidarity through doorknocking, holding public debates, circulating petitions, joining suffrage leagues and writing to a press that frequently knocked them as ugly spinsters. These women had a strong vision for the future, not just on the right for women to vote, but for what social and political transformation could look like.

'The suffragists didn't just walk away when they didn't get it done the first time. They kept recalibrating. They kept regrouping. They kept adapting their strategies,' Tiernan says.

There is a lot to learn from the women who dedicated their lives to the struggle of getting the right to vote. Similarly, there is a lot to be learned from Australia's early democratic achievements, like the establishment of a minimum wage and an aged pension, and compulsory Saturday voting—landmarks that led Australia to be recognised as a model democratic innovator.

In her essay 'Active Citizens, Constructive Answers', Tiernan asks us to look to our shared sense of history to guide us towards the lessons of the past that might be salient now. 'Australia's responses to external shocks,' including pandemics, she writes, 'have always combined capabilities and resources drawn from diverse sectors.

'Such responses were collaborative and purpose-orientated, and reflected a willingness to embrace collective leadership and shared responsibility. They were also relational rather than transactional, reflecting the best traditions of Australian democracy and governance.'

Our shared history served us well in the pandemic.

We saw leadership—if only briefly—from a man who'd been absent during the bushfire crisis. And we saw genuine collaboration and unity between states and territories—regardless of their political leaning—who came together for the common good of the people. The move away from adversarial, conflict-driven, point-scoring politics to politics that was based on problem solving was a breath of fresh air.

We witnessed a government doing its job, if only for a short period of time. The pandemic, in essence, validated the role of government and the importance of trust, not only between citizen and state, but between people. It validated the importance of being part of a truly civil society.

We cannot undo the past thirty or forty years of neoliberal policies, nor unlearn the language that has guided our country. We can't undo market liberalisation. We can't extinguish the vicious media cycle. We can't replant the trees cut down to make way for new apartment blocks. But we can rebuild. We can look forward to ask: what would good government look like? Where could it be found?

The biggest risk we now face is inertia and complacency.

Time will tell whether we experience another wave of the virus. Maybe by the time you read this, what happened in Melbourne in mid-2020 may have well unfolded elsewhere in the country.

'There's a risk this will be like the Global Financial Crisis and that Australians will go, "What? What happened? Thousands of people didn't die and our economy didn't go to hell," so the necessary changes that one would hope to come out of this—a big shift in the policy regime and in the social security safety net and in all these other mechanisms—won't happen. After a few months everything will be back to the way it was before. I do think it's a really significant risk,' Tiernan says.

Along with rampant scepticism about the necessity of the lockdown—which many argued wasn't 'worth it' because far fewer people than predicted died—came the spread of conspiracy theories, most notably that COVID-19 is caused by 5G mobile-phone technology. In mid-May protestors took to the streets of some of Australia's major cities clutching placards that claimed '5G = communism' and

'Covid 1984'. In one of his career highs, the federal government's chief medical officer, Professor Brendan Murphy, had to release a statement assuring Australians that 'turning off your wi-fi will not protect you from COVID-19'.

'What happens when you have inertia and antagonism being much more common than hopefulness and the desire to do things with good intentions?' asks feminist author and activist Eva Cox. 'People look for authoritarian stuff...They look for leadership. They also look for wild beliefs that explain what is going on—so you get all these theories that the pandemic is caused by 5G.

'What really scares me is this conspiracy theory stuff...Go back and look at Germany just before Hitler took over.'

She should know—Cox was born into a Jewish family in Vienna three weeks before the annexation of Austria into Nazi Germany in 1938.

COMMUNITY ORGANISING FOR CHANGE?

Cox's stark warning echoed through my head long afterwards. Her words made me think about how vital it is to harness this moment. We have been afforded the opportunity to rethink the type of society we want to belong to and—importantly—create hope. In order to do so, we need to become conscious that sticking with the status quo is untenable.

This deep awareness is going to have to come from young people—the worst impacted, the least served, and the inheritors of a country in the midst of a climate emergency and on the brink of ecological collapse.

After acknowledging that we want to create a better society, we need to reinvigorate democracy. We must actively empower people to work for the common good. This means going beyond merely saying, 'I stand for change.' It means standing for people to have the agency and organisation to create and shape change. It means we need ideas.

'What can be done and who's going to do it?' asks Tiernan. 'Where's the thinking? Who are the thinkers? I worry that people are so engaged in feeding the machine and doing their work that there's no time for critical reflection. Are we asking people to engage in the wrong way? Should we be getting people to engage at the level of ideas and imagining differently? I think it has to be at the level of ideas because that to me is the biggest gap. I'm looking for people with ideas. And what I see is the same old voices, white males, born in the forties. Excuse me, hello, where is the new and different? This model has been unchallenged for forty years and it's demonstrably failed.'

We might look to the Every Australian Counts campaign, not only for hope, but to see that we are open to big, bold ideas. This campaign was made up of hundreds of thousands of people with disabilities, along with their families and carers, and launched back in 2011. They came together to fight for the establishment of a national system to provide individual, tailored support to disabled people through the National Disability Insurance Scheme (NDIS). The idea had been around since 2008, but it wasn't until 2011 that a public campaign got it the widespread support it needed. Just two years later, in 2013, the NDIS began rolling out across some parts of the country. The scheme is far from perfect, but it shows that we're happy to pay for progressive change out of our own pockets and that, with the right ideas, tremendous change is possible.

•••

I began this chapter exploring the flowering of mutual-aid groups during the pandemic, which gave us a brief insight into what a post-neoliberal world could look like. It was an outpouring from people who wanted to help in ways as varied as dropping off food to neighbours to developing new forms of connection and economy from the ground up. It was the antithesis of competition, and it was inspiring.

Of course, such levels of altruism are not sustainable in the long term without dedicated support. But if this energy were recognised—and valued—it could be harnessed to its full potential.

This begs the question: if we have structures for sustaining bureaucracy and ugly politics, why can't we repurpose that infrastructure to support and sustain the outpouring of energy and dedication that became visible during the pandemic?

When I ask Eva Cox her thoughts about the explosion of mutual-aid groups during the pandemic, she directs me to her 1995 Boyer Lectures, published as *A Truly Civil Society*. Her words may have been spoken twenty-five years ago, but they could have been written today.

Her lectures focus on what binds us: the ties that we call society and community. She argues that there has been far too little attention paid to social capital—'the processes between people which establish networks, norms, social trust and facilitate co-ordination and co-operation for mutual benefit'.

Social capital is important because a strong, active, civil society—one which engenders trust, recognises the common good and embodies 'we' rather than 'I'—enables democracy to thrive. If we trust others as we trust ourselves, we are able to build communities; we are able to collaborate and knit together the fabric of our lives. As Cox writes, 'If most of our experiences enhance our sense of trust and mutuality, allowing us to feel valued and to value others, then social capital increases.'

Trust is a critical part of this because, as Christopher Beem writes in his book *The Necessity of Politics: Reclaiming American Public Life*, 'Trust between individuals thus becomes trust between strangers and trust of a broad fabric of social institutions; ultimately, it becomes a shared set of values, virtues, and expectations within society as a whole.' Without this interaction, he warns, 'trust decays; at a certain point, this decay begins to manifest itself in serious social problems'. Sound familiar?

Cox's lectures reference American political scientist Robert D. Putnam, who is credited with popularising the term 'social capital'. Putnam suggests that we can develop social capital through active relationships. This may be through community groups, neighbourhood centres, local sporting groups or playgroups—all groups that have an egalitarian, voluntaristic structure. Such groups are run democratically—people participate in them because they want to and they are built on the forces that bind us as social beings: trust, reciprocity and mutuality.

What we saw during the pandemic was a huge increase in social capital. The outpouring of support for one another and the proliferation of mutual-aid groups created the space to develop meaningful connection with one another and build on what we have in common rather than using our differences to create fear and competition. #Viralkindess—a social media movement of community care groups across Australia who were supporting neighbours in need during the pandemic—sparked local action nationwide. In Sydney, a group of women connected creatives who'd lost work with essential workers in need of child care. In South Australia, a group of men created an online space to share their mental-health struggles. In Victoria, interpreters and communities banded together to translate health messages into other languages. Such mutual aid helped to reinstate trust in communities by telling stories about who we are, what we want and what is possible. They formed a bridge between the grassroots and political level, creating infrastructure that must be installed if such changes are to be sustained, sustainable and possible.

Now is the time to harness that. It is the time for self-organised community groups to continue to thrive, beyond lockdown. Mutual-aid groups bond us by enabling us to recognise all we have in common. They also enable us to realise there are alternatives; they offer a foreshadowing of what is possible—and what is necessary.

'Why can't we start looking at other ways of measuring the value of things? After all, it's the social that holds society together, not money,' Cox says.

These self-organised groups can also be the basis for local, decentralised democratic projects, from shared transport, to community housing, to food cooperatives. They are member-led and member-organised, and support and facilitate participatory democracy, shared power and collaborative decision-making. At their heart is trust—the cement that glues society together.

Such groups are not only essential to growing social capital—they are essential in a post-COVID-19 world, where, despite people's longing, there will be no return to 'normal'. That is okay, though, because we need a better normal.

Without sweeping changes in the way we do things, the production and distribution of food (80 per cent of the retail grocery market is controlled by two corporations; 2.265 million people are food insecure), housing (140,600 people are on social-housing waitlists;

hundreds of thousands more face rental stress) and education (poverty and disadvantage drive growing inequality in school outcomes) will be even more unequal, more destructive and more unjust than before.

As Putnam writes in his seminal work, *Bowling Alone: The Collapse and Revival of American Community*, 'citizens in civic communities expect and get better government…they are prepared to act collectively to achieve shared goals'.

We can use mutual-aid groups as one way of setting the agenda—as a way of forming the basis for creating the cooperative, collaborative and fair society we want to have.

REINVIGORATING DEMOCRACY

The collapse of faith in our democracy is no accident. It's one of the key goals of neoliberalism. Our retreat from politics—our disengagement from and lack of interest in it—is perilous, because it has made it easier for politicians to pander to the already rich and powerful, and for decisions to be made in the interests of the few rather than the majority.

One of the most glaring examples to come to light during the pandemic was the make-up of the National COVID-19 Commission Advisory Board, a publicly funded body set up to advise the government on how to mitigate the economic and social impacts of the novel coronavirus. The board is chaired by Nev Power, a former Fortescue Metals chief and current board member at gas company Strike Energy. The group, which includes other private-sector leaders such as former long-time boss of the transport and logistics company Toll Holdings, Paul Little, recommended the government make sweeping changes to 'create the market' for gas and build fossil-fuel infrastructure that would operate for decades.

We urgently need to find ways to re-engage people in politics and democratic decision-making that goes beyond the scope of mutual-aid groups. People must be galvanised from their current malaise to become active citizens. This is not about reinventing democracy; it's about reinvigorating it.

Professor Mark Evans is the director of Democracy 2025, a project of the Museum of Australian Democracy and the University of Canberra, which is focused on rebuilding trust between government and citizens by driving a national conversation that looks at both the strengths and weaknesses of our democratic practice. The project has been named Democracy 2025 because if nothing is done by 2025, and current trends continue, fewer than 10 per cent of Australians will trust their politicians and political institutions. This will have devastating effects. We will have a more ineffective and illegitimate government, and the disparity between rich and poor, and poor and poorer, will be even wider than it is today. To reverse this trend, Evans tells me, the way forward is democratic renewal in the form of a collaborative approach to problem solving, one led by citizens and in which the government is a partner.

Hollo agrees that the answer to this entrenched problem is more representative democracy. More specifically, a democracy that cultivates 'ethics and mechanisms of participation, interdependence, interconnection, resilience that actively bring the community in'.

'Australians are supportive of democracy. We don't want to get rid of democracy, we like the idea of democracy, we just don't trust democracy,' he says. 'There are people who try to paint the situation as "democracy doesn't work", and "we can't trust democracy so therefore we should head towards authoritarianism", but what I'm saying is the opposite. We want democracy, we need democracy, and the answer is more democracy.'

There are numerous examples here in Australia that we can look to for inspiration to grow new and reimagined democracies.

'Strong communities have a shared vision about how they want to be with each other, how they want to interact and their vision for now, the middle and the longer-term.'

'Being involved in decision-making.'

'People don't voice their concerns because they don't know where to go.'

'Focus on our strengths and also on the richness of our diversity.'

'We demand a better standard of behaviour from our elected representatives.'

'Frustrated that we don't have a choice and a voice.'

'Feeling disenfranchised.'

These are the thoughts and feelings of some of the 425 people who, in 2013, participated in something known as Kitchen Table Conversations in the electorate of Indi in Victoria.

The idea is simple: groups of ten people—friends, neighbours, family and colleagues—get together at the pub, the yoga studio, at a cafe, to have a discussion. The conversations are guided by some broad questions such as, 'What are the particular issues within the Indi electorate that concern you?', 'What is good political representation?' and 'What makes a stronger relationship between people and elected representatives?'.

In 2012, the Voices for Indi committee was set up by eleven residents of the electorate who wanted to strengthen the relationship between community and policymakers, and to develop leadership with a vision that represents and delivers for the people of Indi. They envisioned a deliberative democracy that was based on civic engagement, respect and ideas.

Through Kitchen Table Conversations, along with faith and widespread community engagement, the grassroots campaign endorsed Cathy McGowan as an independent for the 2013 election. Against the odds, the campaign unseated the longstanding Liberal member, Sophie Mirabella. It was the only seat lost by the Liberals when Tony Abbott's government came to office.

Not only was McGowan re-elected in 2016, but when she decided to retire at the 2019 election, it was because she was confident that an independent successor, chosen by Voices for Indi, would be able to retain the seat. And she was right.

In early January 2019, Dr Helen Haines was endorsed by Voices for Indi as her potential successor. In an unprecedented community political process, Voices for Indi invited hundreds of registered campaign volunteers to a meeting to determine a 'succession process'. More than two hundred volunteers from McGowan's past election campaigns handpicked Haines as their next candidate from a panel of three nominees who'd responded to community callouts for potential contenders in the newspaper. The process involved putting candidates through six hours of questioning and deliberation. The decision was reached by consensus of all participants.

'What's really quite striking about Cathy McGowan is that it's the first time in Australian political history that an independent has in effect handed over to another independent,' Nicholas Gruen, public intellectual and former chair of the Australian Centre for Social Innovation, says of Haines's win.

The participatory Voices for Indi campaign that elected McGowan twice and then made history by nominating Dr Haines to succeed her signalled the responsiveness of the community to being involved in co-designing mechanisms that enable democratic participation, representation and accountability. It's also a strong example of bridging the divide between community-driven, grass-roots political activity and representation, and the formal political structures that are visible at the national level. Connecting the two layers—feeding the effects of one into the mix of the other—is one of the missing steps between community activity and genuine political enfranchisement.

Other Australian jurisdictions have also experimented with citizens' juries and assemblies, which are, in some parts of the world, fast gathering steam. Australia's most famous example is South Australia, which randomly selected citizens to resolve the question of whether or not to build a nuclear waste dump in the state. In early 2016, the first citizens' jury was held, which brought together fifty randomly selected South Australian citizens over two weekends to discuss the findings of the Nuclear Fuel Cycle Royal Commission Report, come to a judgment and make recommendations to the government. Jurors were chosen from a pool of twenty-five thousand randomly selected households, which received invitations outlining the point of the process and how it worked. Even the premier at the time, Jay Weatherill, who supported the citizens' jury, received an invite.

Later that year, the jury met again with an additional three hundred South Australians to answer the question: 'Under what circumstances, if any, could South Australia pursue the opportunity to store and dispose of nuclear waste from other countries?' Against the will of both the government and opposition, the jury delivered a loud and clear verdict: No. Under no circumstances would this be acceptable. The idea was shut down.

Gruen, who has been involved in citizens' juries, says that the overwhelming majority of those who take part in such a deliberative process describe it as a 'positive or very positive experience'. People feel a great sense of responsibility and are grateful for the opportunity to deliberate on fundamental societal issues. Remarkably, he tells me, up to half of the participants have described participating in such a deliberation as 'life changing'.

'You know, this is how human beings evolved,' he says. 'We're the problem-solving species. We're the arguing species. That's how we did it.'

Gruen also cites a City of Melbourne example from 2015. Forty-three people, who were selected using the random stratified sample process to reflect the city's demographics, were brought together to deliberate and make decisions as to how the council should spend $5 billion over ten years. The jury was asked one question: 'How can we remain one of the most liveable cities in the world while addressing our future financial challenges?' Over six weekends, the jury came up with recommendations for the council on its spending and revenue strategy. Ten of the eleven recommendations are being implemented.

Interestingly enough, three of the participants were so inspired by the process that they went on to stand for local government.

'Now, I don't know the statistics, but I'm pretty sure that five per cent of people don't stand for Melbourne Council at the next opportunity they get,' Gruen says.

The City of Sydney followed a similar approach in 2019. It brought together fifty randomly selected Sydneysiders to review more than 2500 submissions for ideas for the future of the city. The jury identified eight concepts to realise the community's vision for 2050. The first was participatory governance: 'We want a new model of governance that genuinely engages citizens in decision-making on all levels, and is responsive and adaptable,' their report reads.

Perhaps the most famous example of citizens' juries and assemblies delivering change was the process to remove the constitutional ban on abortion in Ireland in 2016. The citizens' assembly brought together a hundred randomly selected individuals over five weekends to deliberate on this highly controversial topic. Recommending liberalisation, their decision went on to be ratified in a national referendum and then enshrined into law. Louise Caldwell, who was a member of the assembly, wrote in the *Guardian* that the experience made her feel 'empowered and informed—it gave me the language and skills to have difficult discussions. I think most people want to find things we agree on and to discover common ground—through this we can always learn new ways to go forward.'

'If you come along to a citizen assembly, honest to God, it will reinvigorate you. It's one of those things where you realise, "Wow, this works,"' says author and academic Tim Dunlop, who has extensively studied and written about citizens' juries and assemblies. 'These people...have never been involved in the political process before, they've washed their hands of the political process, and have become very cynical and disengaged, but when you put them in that situation, they just come out flying. They have such a positive experience and it's pretty much universal.'

The key to citizens' assemblies, Dunlop says, is that they put in place structures that reward deliberation and cooperation, rather than the kind of abuse we see yelled across chambers on almost every day parliament sits.

'We really need structural change. It can't just be begging politicians to be better,' he says.

Inclusive participation in democratic deliberation allows ordinary people to have a say. It means a variety of voices can be heard rather than just the elected representative who, in many cases, is voted in because she or he is the least worst option.

The willingness of people to take part, and the overwhelmingly positive feedback people involved in citizens' juries have given, indicate that Australians are not apathetic about their political system—we just need the opportunity to enter the debate.

'These participatory, community-building projects, from sharing groups to citizens' assemblies, are the next big struggle for franchise,' Hollo writes in the *Guardian*. 'They directly confront disenfranchisement by directly re-enfranchising people—enabling us to play a real role in determining our future.'

Citizens' assemblies could also be extended beyond a random selection of participants and engage an even broader audience. Harnessing digital technology, through myGov or a similar online hub, we could conduct citizen polls on the priorities identified by the deliberative forums to test the recommendations with the general population. It would be interesting to see who—and how many—would want to participate in such deliberation. If it was publicised far and wide—and made easy to access—I'm guessing it would be a hell of a lot of people.

Through the growth of the digital sphere, such online democracy platforms could bring governments closer to citizens and enable policies to be created in a way that is more of a reflection of what we believe in as a nation. It could also help to bridge the rural–urban divide.

The idea of digital democracy in any sense of the word isn't merely about online engagement; it's about embedding systems and processes within governments to enable a wide range of voices to be heard, regardless of the way in which people choose to participate.

I think the greatest lesson we can take away from the experiments with deliberative democracy is that formalising these processes as part of the democratic infrastructure is certainly worthy of pursuit.

•••

When you think about a jury, in the legal sense, it largely conjures up words like trust, transparency and objectivity. Jurors for a court case are chosen by sortition—the selection of citizens at random from the citizenry—so we trust that they aren't corrupt or manipulative. We also trust that jurors aren't driven by the desire for power or money or ego and that the unanimous jury verdict represents the view of the people.

Juries are, perhaps, the only democratic institution that hasn't witnessed a collapse in social trust in recent years.

Sortition—which moves between thinking, deliberating and power—goes all the way back to ancient Athens, where it was used to combat the threat of aristocratic families fighting among themselves to reinstate an oligarchy.

With interest in sortition across the world thriving, numerous books, articles and papers have been published about the design of deliberative bodies populated by people who are selected by lottery. Some could work in Australia; others may not.

Some academics suggest sortition should replace the state altogether, while others argue that deliberative bodies chosen by sortition could replace existing legislative chambers such as the Australian Senate. At the heart of this multitude of options is people power:

giving ordinary citizens the power to make decisions about the type of society they want to live in.

I ask Nicholas Gruen what his ideal would be—if we could make citizens' juries or the like a permanent part of our constitution.

His ideal is a People's Chamber, which would comprise 227 people—the number of parliamentarians we have. Among the 227 people, at least one would come from every electorate in Australia, randomised with representative random selection. This means that we would keep clicking until we get a mix of ordinary people from all electorates with at least 48 per cent men or women who represent the right proportion of regional and rural and city. The people would be chosen for six-year non-renewable terms, with sixty-seven new people appointed every two years.

The People's Chamber would have the power to delay but not block legislation passed by the House of Representatives, similar to the House of Lords in the United Kingdom. The People's Chamber would also be able to propose legislation. Having the ability to propose legislation could reinvigorate the search for policy options and solutions to problems that had been condemned to the 'too hard' basket—such as introducing a sugar tax to curb rising obesity levels.

As discussed in Tim Dunlop's book *The Future of Everything*, this idea could go even further by replacing the Australian Senate members by sortition while retaining the powers it currently has to review and reject legislation. Gruen suggests, though, another power for a People's Chamber: the opportunity to 'compel a secret ballot of the other chamber(s) on the matter in question'. If a secret ballot failed to resolve the matter in question, a mechanism similar to section 57 of our constitution, which is used for resolving a deadlock between the House of Representatives and the Senate, would be invoked.

If, after three months, the deadlock between the chambers remained, the matter would be resolved in a joint sitting between them. That is, both houses would sit and deliberate and vote. This means the lower house could not ignore the advice of the People's Chamber—something that could happen if it was set up purely as an advisory group.

Gruen recognises that his idea is ambitious, but he doesn't believe that there's anything unimaginable about it. Neither do I. 'I just want to get enough theory out there to get the starter motor going,' he tells me.

We could start small, with citizens themselves, using donations from the public or businesses, forming their own people's chamber. We could even begin it through crowdfunding. Gruen asks us to imagine a body of 101 people chosen at random from a relevant population, and given the resources to fund research and call expert witnesses.

'One might sit four times a year for nine days—encompassing one week and the weekend on either side of it. The chamber would deliberate on the choices before the electorate at large...They would deliberate on the parties' policies, they would invite spokespeople for those parties or others to address them and help them deliberate on the merits of the choices to be made by the people. They would also... work on the brief communiques explaining the case for and against various options together with how the body voted on them.

'I think this could have an electrifying effect on political business as usual.'

I believe so too. By putting ordinary people at the heart of power, we not only transform the notion of power itself, but we transform ugly politics and return it to a space where ordinary citizens are empowered, engaged and, importantly, represented.

•••

In his book *The Great Leveler: Violence and the History of Inequality from the Stone Age to the Twenty-First Century*, Walter Scheidel points out that only four things over the course of history have been capable of destroying the fortunes of the rich and thus led to a more equal society. Dubbed the 'Four Horsemen', these are: mass-mobilisation warfare, transformative revolutions, state collapse and catastrophic plagues.

We didn't need to wait for a catastrophic plague to move towards creating a more equal, just Australia, but nevertheless it is a powerful force for change. The pandemic has afforded us a huge opportunity to reimagine the type of country we want to belong to.

With the government's newfound respect for knowledge, expertise, evidence-based policy and collective leadership, Australia became one of the world's most successful countries in dealing with the COVID-19 pandemic.

But as quickly as we witnessed a transformational moment, that consensus has all but vanished. We cannot let this deter us. For all that we have witnessed our communities to be capable of, we need to continue to press forward in wielding our own power in new and innovative ways. We need to cultivate and nurture ground-up forms of government to enable them to bear upon pre-existing democratic structures in order to shift the infrastructure of power.

There is no doubt that to move from where we are to where we want to be is going to involve some messy untangling and a lot of grit. But we need to have the confidence to trust ourselves over those who tell us we are disengaged and indifferent and lack the experience—and desire—to participate.

We also need to have the courage to face societal fissures and divisions on an individual, one-to-one basis, within communal political settings. People coming from different sections of society to discuss contentious topics is empowering, but it also requires great courage, resilience and openness. Being strong and trusting in the foundations of community is necessary—the courage to be truly civic-minded in a genuinely civil society. For every time we do this, we will defy a system that tells us that we are better apart.

By starting small, we can build the momentum to take on more audacious reforms, such as creating a People's Chamber. And we need to. We *can* build the institutions that reflect our values—fairness, inclusion, reciprocity—which will not only give people a voice, but empower them.

We don't know what the future holds, but we know there will be more crises—ones that we cannot yet see or imagine. By coming together for the common good, we can bridge the gulf between citizen and governments and create a truly civil society—one that is stronger in every sense of the word—together. Creating this life in common, whereby we share everything from power to food to government itself, is something we need to not just imagine but create. To do so, we must realise that the alternatives out there—the ones discussed in this chapter and far beyond—are possible.

In the words of Welsh Marxist theorist Raymond Williams: 'To be truly radical is to make hope possible rather than despair convincing.'

2 | WELFARE

> 'It is not great wealth in a few individuals that proves a country is prosperous, but great general wealth evenly distributed among the people.'
>
> VICTORIA WOODHULL, THE FIRST WOMAN TO RUN FOR PRESIDENT OF THE UNITED STATES, IN 1872

In 2011, six thousand men, women and children in eight villages in the central Indian state of Madhya Pradesh began receiving a basic income. It would transform their lives.

Madhya Pradesh is in the heart of India, where the majority of its 74-million-strong population are dependent on agriculture. It's also a state with a large Scheduled Castes and Scheduled Tribes population—people who are the most socio-economically disadvantaged and denigrated in India, if not the world. They are people who are largely mobile, migrating to neighbouring states with the wheat, soya bean and potato seasons. They often don't get paid in cash, but in bucket loads of the crops they plough.

The villages—at least the ones I've visited—generally comprise a series of thatched huts with bamboo roofs and a communal well where people get their water when it's available. In the monsoon months, the grass is electric green and the afternoon downpours so frequent, so intense, that they flood villages. In the dry months, the reddened land is sparse, punctuated with tall, wilted trees that look depressed. In April and May, the almost-summer heat is oppressive.

The pilot—which ran for eighteen months—was innovative compared to similar programs previously run in different parts of the world in that it was universal, unconditional and individual. That meant that every single adult and child received a monthly income with no strings attached. The only requirement was that people had to open a bank account in order to receive the money. For children under the age of eighteen, payments went to the mother or designated guardian.

As a randomised control trial, the experiences of people receiving basic income in the eight villages was tracked against twelve similar villages where nobody received it. It was the first time that a project like this was subject to such detailed assessment in the country.

The results were profound. Food insecurity more than halved, as did levels of malnutrition. By the end of the project, the proportion of children with normal weight for age had increased from 39 per cent to 59 per cent—an improvement that was double that in the control villages. Malnutrition is rife in India, fuelled not only by a lack of nutritious food, but by structural inequality—poor sanitation, poor education, poverty. It is just another problem on top of many others.

The basic income enabled families to improve their living conditions to a standard that could be described as basic: they installed latrines, repaired roofs destroyed in the monsoon rains, and added mosquito nets to protect from malaria, dengue, chikungunya and the other mosquito-borne diseases.

The basic income also helped to keep teenage girls in school who might overwise have been forced out for marriage or work; it helped the disabled more than others, women more than men, and Scheduled Caste households more than high-Caste ones. It also unexpectedly reduced bonded labour.

A common criticism of welfare systems around the world is that 'handing out' money to citizens will make people lazy by disincentivising them to work. Really, what these critics are saying is that the recipients do not deserve this 'free' money—it is their fault they are poor and out of work. It reminds me of the dangerous lie peddled for decades that those with HIV/AIDS are promiscuous and therefore to blame for their infection. It's a classist attitude, riddled with dark undertones of discrimination, particularly here in Australia.

This project—like so many others—strongly refutes that belief. In Madhya Pradesh, having a basic income led to more work and labour, raised productivity and—in particular, yet not surprisingly—saw a drastic rise in secondary, self-employed work. One unanticipated result was that the emancipatory value of the basic income far exceeded the monetary value. In other words, the basic income gave people the freedom to create new opportunities for themselves that would ultimately transform their lives for the better. As economist Guy Standing, who led the trial funded by UNICEF, writes: 'Emancipatory universalism has been sacrificed everywhere... In sum, basic income grants could be a vital part of a twenty-first-century social protection system...Old-style paternalism must be rejected and a new progressive system constructed.'

'Free money works. Already, research has correlated unconditional cash disbursements with reductions in crime, child mortality, malnutrition, teenage pregnancy, and truancy, and with improved school performance, economic growth, and gender equality,' historian Rutger Bregman writes in *Utopia for Realists: And How We Can Get There.*

The project's positive outcomes left me wondering what long-term impacts a universal basic income could have on the caste system in India, how it might reduce the stigma attached to the 'poor' and others in society who are considered a burden, and how it could improve health and education outcomes. Which in turn got me thinking about how a universal basic income could help dismantle our own class system in Australia. It also prompted me to consider the effect it could have on gender equality—how a universal basic income could serve as a tool to value women's unpaid domestic work.

In the lead-up to India's 2019 election, the country's main opposition leader, Rahul Gandhi, told the nation that if he were elected, he would introduce a guaranteed income to 250 million of the country's poorest citizens. While strongman Narendra Modi was unsurprisingly re-elected for another term, the fact that the world's second most populous country could even consider introducing a basic income testifies to its growing legitimacy. I also use India as an example—as opposed to other countries like Canada and Finland, which have also trialled basic incomes—because we here in Australia think that we cannot relate to the poor, that poverty in India is too distant from our own lived experiences. India feels too far away, too exotic, too *other* for similarities to be drawn—when in fact that's not the case at all.

•••

In March 2020, as COVID-19 took hold in Australia, the government announced a range of sweeping measures to prop up the economy and support households as we lived through a time of anxiety and fear and uncertainty.

As the country went into lockdown and hundreds of thousands of people suddenly found themselves unemployed overnight, the government introduced the JobSeeker Payment. In replacing the Newstart Allowance unemployment scheme, JobSeeker became the main income support both for people who'd lost their jobs due to the pandemic and for those who were already unemployed. At a maximum of $1,115.70 per fortnight (excluding rent assistance and family payments), the payment was almost double that of the Newstart Allowance and was seen as vital to keeping Australians out of poverty. (It has since been slashed.) It was the largest increase to social security benefits in Australia's history.

Not long afterwards, the government announced the JobKeeper Payment, a wage subsidy scheme that delivered a payment of $1500 per fortnight to businesses significantly affected by COVID-19 (which again has since been cut). The purpose of the $70 billion fund was to maintain employment levels, even when people weren't actually working.

Under these far-reaching changes to the welfare system, the government also mandated that the application process would be streamlined; prospective welfare recipients would no longer need to attend a Centrelink office to complete their claim. The overly complex and bureaucratic system was apparently going to be a thing of the past.

But the day after the prime minister announced the JobSeeker scheme, it became apparent the government was not prepared. Across the country, queues outside Centrelink offices snaked along streets and around shuttered restaurants, gyms and libraries, as the myGov website crashed and calls to the phone 'help lines' went unanswered. The nation's social security system went into meltdown.

'My bad for not realising the sheer scale of the decision on Sunday night by national leaders that literally saw hundreds of thousands, maybe a million, people unemployed overnight,' Government Services Minister Stuart Robert told Sydney radio station 2GB.

Hospitality was one of the sectors hit hardest. The owners and employees of cafes, bars, restaurants—and all the businesses that supply produce to them—found their lives completely upended.

'All the farmers who were supplying restaurants completely had the rugs pulled out from underneath them when hospitality shut down,' says Tammi Jonas, who runs a farm with her family near Daylesford in Victoria. 'If you were in that medium- to small-scale size, that was your main market and overnight it was gone.'

As the government abandoned its neoliberal strictures on fiscal restraint, it also declared changes to child care to enable essential workers to continue working. Child care in Australia—which is expensive, and a drain on family expenditure that leaves parents with the impossible choice of working to pay for child care or staying home to save on the expense—was now free.

As I watched the prime minister make the announcement at the beginning of April, I was gobsmacked. I imagine many others also were. Had the Liberal Party introduced such policies prior to the pandemic, they would have been pilloried as 'dangerous socialism', wrote Richard Flanagan in the *New York Times.*

'For too long the conservative side of politics has portrayed those receiving welfare as being a freeloading underclass,' says Secretary of the Australian Council of Trade Unions Sally McManus. 'This crisis has torn the curtain back on that nasty myth. Hopefully that has given many people pause for thought that others who have sought welfare assistance have had to deal with circumstances just as challenging.'

The policies saw us return to some extent to our purported values of fairness, inclusion and communality. Along with our enviable health response, these policies enabled us to weather the pandemic with a degree of trust in our government.

'It probably is fair to say that there has been the type of change in three weeks inside the award system that you might otherwise wait thirty years to see,' Industrial Relations Minister Christian Porter told reporters.

But while some suggested this wave of new support could become our new normal, the prime minister quickly reminded us this would not be the case. If we needed proof that the old ways were not being abandoned, the deliberate exclusion of public universities from JobKeeper was it. We were told we shouldn't get used to the idea of a government delivering welfare support at a level above the poverty line as JobSeeker and JobKeeper payments were cut. And forget about child care—a monster multi-billion-dollar industry—being free and enabling more women to join or rejoin the workforce. What a fantastical idea.

Before long, Scott Morrison assured us that the raft of crisis-related economic support would 'snap back' to their old arrangements to avoid an ongoing budget drain. The prime minister told the press club that it was vital to get the Australian economy 'out of ICU' and 'off the medication' of government support 'before it becomes too accustomed to it'.

As the offensive use of medical metaphors (while Australians died of the virus in ICUs) and the term 'snapback' became the rhetoric in which to speak about economic recovery, it was a stark reminder that this was temporary: there was an end date. But while you can decide when to end a stimulus package, you can't decide when to end a pandemic.

'Much of the rhetorical power of neoliberalism arose from the way it laid claim to words like "efficiency", "productivity" and "growth", distorted them, and then injected them back into public debate in the most confusing ways,' Richard Denniss, chief economist at the Australia Institute, writes in his Quarterly Essay, *Dead Right*:

> For example, once you convince people that government spending is wasteful, it is easy to argue that any cuts in government spending are efficient. It's not a complicated trick, but it is audacious. And it clearly works...If there is one thing that neoliberals really seem to believe, it is that reducing the budget deficit is very, very important. Except when it isn't.

While temporary in nature, the sweeping reforms to the welfare system in response to the pandemic laid bare not only the punitive nature of our social security system but the farcical level of Newstart's forty-dollars-a-day allowance. It revealed the system as not fit for our complex labour market and the precarious nature of work.

The pandemic also exposed just how quickly any one of us could be the one requiring government assistance. Maybe those on welfare weren't dole bludgers sitting at home binge-watching Netflix; maybe they simply needed help.

It was also revelatory in that it showed that drastic policy changes can literally happen overnight.

Fundamentally, it reinvigorated the argument for a universal basic income, the revolutionary policy that is not only necessary, but possible.

'I think the coronavirus has made it more obvious that a universal basic income is a good idea,' says Dr Jeremy Baskin, senior fellow at the Melbourne School of Government. 'We need a system that treats all citizens as having some basic fundamental rights to economic security.'

AUSTRALIA, LAND OF THE FAIR GO

At the turn of the twentieth century, Australia was recognised as both a model democratic practitioner and a political innovator. It 'adopted policies that promoted economic participation and inclusion through education, horizontal fiscal equalisation, needs-based wages and targeted welfare', writes Anne Tiernan in her essay 'Active Citizens, Constructive Answers'.

The precursor to this was the 1890s economic depression, which led to the rise of trade unions and Labor parties that ultimately pushed for welfare reform. Then, in 1900, both NSW and Victoria enacted legislation introducing non-contributory pensions for those aged sixty. Not long afterwards, the Commonwealth government introduced a national aged pension, a disability allowance and a national maternity allowance. Such policies gave rise to a new nation that offered opportunities for all, not just the privileged. (The catch was that these policies only applied to white Australians.)

It was during the Second World War that Australia under a Labor government created a welfare state by enacting a range of national schemes that included a wife's allowance, unemployment and sickness benefits, and a widow's allowance. The welfare state was devised not only to prevent people from falling into poverty—the opposite of today, where recipients face an uphill battle to survive on negligible support, let alone pull themselves up and out of dependence—but to ensure quality public education, affordable housing, shorter working hours, a legislated basic wage, national health services and equality of opportunity.

When servicemen returned home from war, the battles still fresh in their minds, and people displaced from Europe arrived in Australia by boat, they came to a country that was committed to social protection 'through a policy focus on full employment, the "living wage", affordable housing and other government interventions that aimed to protect vulnerable groups from exogenous shocks', as Tiernan outlines. With that commitment to social protection was also the assumption that if you could work, you would. The policy focus on full employment and a 'living wage' was there for a reason.

'There's a long history of the Australian welfare system since Federation being obsessed with the idea that the deserving people are the people that contribute to society,' says Dr Elise Klein, senior lecturer of public policy at the Crawford School at the Australian National University (ANU).

'And so, this idea of the worker: if you have a job you're seen as a worthy citizen and anyone outside of that is not,' she says. 'The social-security system has continually been used through Australian settler history as a way to define who is deserving and who is not.'

We don't need to look far to see evidence of this—the aged pension was set up to reward people who had contributed to society throughout their lives; the veteran's payment similarly rewarded people who'd put their lives on the line for the country. Neither payment underwent the type of scrutiny that unemployment benefits or parenting payments did.

Interestingly, by the 1970s, the government had already acknowledged that the existing social-security system was unnecessarily complicated. Means tests for different payments conflicted and anomalies proliferated, leading to 'a perplexing range of benefits which have developed in a spasmodic way', according to Bill Hayden, the minister for social security in the newly elected Whitlam Government in 1973.

'The New Labour [sic] Government hopes to completely scrap the present confusing system of pension and Social Security benefits and replace it with a more simply administered and easily understood system of guaranteed income,' he said.

But in the 1980s, social policy took a back seat to new economic goals. The 'fair go' deal was no longer about the collective; it was about individualised competitive opportunities. Dr Klein explains: 'In the 1980s, there was a neoliberal shift—the ideological idea that you have to be your own business and you have to conduct yourself to be economically efficient. So, if you're failing, poverty is seen as an individual behavioural deficiency rather than a structural problem with capitalism.'

Such an attitude has prevailed, infiltrating society to the extent that the colloquial term 'dole bludger' is typically used to speak about those who do not have a job—those who are also described as lazy, underserving, useless citizens. Our spirit of mateship has been warped, reduced to dobbing in alleged 'dole bludgers', like we were encouraged to dob in people flouting the COVID-19 lockdown rules.

The government might speak about our culture of mateship, fairness and inclusion, but our unemployment benefits are among the stingiest in the developed world. More than that, there are so many hoops to jump through in our welfare system that, as Tim Dunlop writes in his book *The Future of Everything*, recipients have been turned 'into among the most surveilled citizens in the country'.

'The cynic in me can't help but think that successive governments—having demonised welfare recipients—felt no compunction in leaving them to languish below the line,' McManus tells me.

These problems are not simply logistical; they are ideological. The welfare system makes people feel that they are worthless, that they are failures. In stark contrast to the supposed love of liberty at the heart of neoliberalism, the way the state makes welfare participants totally dependent on the government shows that there is no sense of freedom about it.

Take, for instance, the mutual obligations Australians have to fulfil to receive the JobSeeker Payment in all parts of the country bar Victoria to 'help you find a job':

> Do all the tasks and activities listed in your Job Plan (attending appointments with an employment services provider or us; job searches, including looking for work and applying for jobs; doing Work for the Dole; other approved activities such as study, training, paid or voluntary work); go to appointments with your employment services provider; complete and report your job searches; accept any offer of suitable paid work.
>
> If you don't meet your mutual obligation requirements, suspensions, demerits or financial penalties may apply.

Judging need based on a binary way of thinking (employed vs unemployed, for example) results in processes that are complex and punitive, and which seemingly have zero insight into the realities people face day-to-day. It has gone so far that former Labor minister turned Commissioner of the Australian Charities and Not-for-profits Commission (ACNC) Dr Gary Johns has even argued that people—more specifically, women—who receive unemployment benefits should have to take contraception as a condition of payment.

As then leader of the opposition Tony Abbott said in 2011:

> Sometimes governments have to be firm to be fair. Allowing people to stay on welfare when there is work they can reasonably do is the kindness that kills. It's the misguided compassion that eventually breaks down the social fabric...Encouraging more people into work...is likely to improve the country's morale and to help people feel more comfortable in their own skins...It's a good social policy as well as an important economic advance.

Such 'kindness' is not the type that kills; a vindictive system that keeps people in poverty is. The average age of a person on Newstart is forty-five. The fastest growing cohort of people on unemployment benefits is over fifty-five. We have an ageing population increasingly unable to find work, yet the government has for decades kept the Newstart Allowance at a level below the poverty line, and has continued to tout the lie that the unemployed are young and otiose.

In Australia, inequality is spiralling out of control. While inequality can be looked at through multiple prisms, such as health and education outcomes, at its heart is income and wealth.

According to the University of New South Wales and the Australian Council of Social Service, the highest 20 per cent of income earners in the country live in households with five times as much income as the lowest 20 per cent. Wealth inequality, meanwhile, continues to increase. The average wealth of the highest 20 per cent rose by 53 per cent from 2003 to 2016, while the lowest 20 per cent declined by 9 per cent. The university found that 63 per cent of households where someone receives the Newstart Allowance have the lowest 5 per cent of incomes in the country.

'In short, those at the bottom of the income distribution are being left further and further behind, not just by those at the top, but by those in full-time work,' writes Denniss in *Dead Right*. 'And the unemployment benefit hasn't increased in real terms for twenty years.'

Not only do wealthier Australians live better than the less privileged among us, they live longer. A 2019 study on health inequality from the University of Melbourne found that the average gap in life expectancy between the bottom 20 per cent of the population and the top 20 per cent is now six years and growing. For people in the lowest 10 per cent of the population, it is ten years.

By peddling the lie that one of the wealthiest nations on the planet couldn't possibly afford to provide those in need with a level of services that equate to an adequate standard of living, neoliberalism has created deepening rifts in our increasingly unequal society.

'We just spent billions on JobKeeper and JobSeeker,' Denniss tells me. 'We made child care free. We could always do it. People in government just didn't want to.'

'Of course,' I say. 'So how can we make this change permanent?'

'Well, by firstly understanding that it was always affordable, and everything we were told was a lie and if we want to keep it, we can.'

Dr Klein echoes Denniss. 'The social security system was set up to stop people from falling into poverty, but it now actually forces people into poverty,' she says. 'Through programs like Newstart Allowance and cashless debit cards, all these programs are actually bringing people into poverty or increasing their likelihood of ending up in poverty. The social security system is not fit for purpose anymore.

'I really hope the government does not wait until things get really, really bad in order for them to make the right decision to provide people with an economic floor to stand on that's unconditional and dignified.'

MAKING A UNIVERSAL BASIC INCOME A REALITY

So, what exactly is a universal basic income, and how does it work? I'm going to use the straightforward definition offered by the Basic Income Earth Network (BIEN), the largest UBI advocacy group in the world. It defines it as a 'periodic cash payment unconditionally delivered to all on an individual basis, without means-test or work requirement'.

The three key elements of a UBI are that it is adequate, universal and unconditional. That means that every citizen receives a wage that is enough to keep them out of poverty. No questions asked. No judgments made.

By being unconditional, that means no one has to fulfil any obligations in order to receive it. That means that no one would need to enter into a Job Plan, undergo a drug test, or participate in trainings or workshops, and that no woman could ever be forced to take contraception in exchange for money.

By being universal, it means that someone who is a single, stay-at-home parent is treated the same as billionaire Gina Rinehart—there are no means tests. It would be paid to all adult citizens regardless of need. It would be paid at the same rate to people with or without jobs;

to people with dependents or without; and to people with disabilities and those without.

And by being adequate, it means the payment is set at a level that is enough to protect citizens against poverty. Depending on the model, universal basic income payments would not necessarily replace all other income support payments. Instead, they could be used in conjunction with other targeted payments such as rent assistance and disability payments.

The fact that the payment is periodic—say, fortnightly or weekly—is critical, because the regularity provides ongoing financial stability, and the ability and freedom to plan. The stress this would alleviate is immeasurable. And because UBI is delivered to the individual rather than to households or families, it recognises individual freedom and, in doing so, has huge emancipatory value—just as the pilot project in the Indian state of Madhya Pradesh showed.

The idea is that a UBI provides a safety net that, unlike the system we have today, doesn't propel people into poverty or enmesh them in its pernicious cycle. A UBI is not a panacea, but it is one solution to a range of problems we face, economic, political and social. It doesn't remove the need to address other major problems that policy has failed to solve—namely, affordable housing and child care. Similarly, we must ensure that a UBI is not seen by right-libertarians as the golden opportunity to disrupt and dismantle the welfare state and force us to buy essential needs, such as education, health, housing and public transport, in the private market.

UBI is not a new, radical idea. It quickly gathered momentum and moved into mainstream public debate after the deep recession in the wake of the Global Financial Crisis, which saw mass job losses and high unemployment in many developed countries. As the world continues to grapple with the COVID-19 pandemic and its destructive fallout, UBI has been brought back into the spotlight as countries around the world face growing hardship and the worst recession in decades.

In response to mass job losses, in June 2020 Spain's government introduced a basic monthly income for struggling families. The government's decision rekindled an idea that had been tossed around the European Union for more than two decades: a pan-EU minimum income. At the time of writing, Portugal, Spain and Italy have joined forces to put forward the idea in the hope that EU governments will come together to hash out how it would be funded, the income amount and eligibility. In the face of growing uncertainty about our present and future—economically, socially, politically, ecologically—it has the potential to transform the lives of millions of the bloc's almost half a billion population.

Back home in Australia, while we have fared measurably better than many of our allies near and far, the raft of economic measures the government installed in the face of mass job losses and months-long lockdowns has not only given credence to a UBI but stimulated a wider discussion about inequality.

'A UBI provides a floor from which you cannot fall,' author and academic Tim Dunlop says. 'In terms of COVID-19, just think how much better off we would have all been if that floor existed. We would not have had to go through all this angst over losing jobs because at least we would have had this guaranteed minimum income that we would have all been getting no matter what we were all doing. It would have made us a lot more resilient to something like the coronavirus. We need to get it in place because it's going to happen again.'

Not only has the virus led to more than a million deaths and hundreds of millions of job losses, it has also fuelled growing anxiety over our collective future on this planet. Ecological reality has made itself felt, its presence omnipresent. The capitalistic belief that the free market will take care of us, and that we are separate from and superior to the natural world, has collapsed in the face of this pandemic. The novel coronavirus has forced us to grapple with fundamental questions, questions that perhaps we should have been asking ourselves long before they felt like an existential, imminent threat. Climate change will make pandemics like COVID-19 more likely because of warming temperatures, biodiversity loss, erratic rainfall and the like.

Now we need to be asking ourselves: is my job pandemic-proof for the next one? How can I best protect myself and my family? Where to go? What to do? Where is safest? Do I have enough savings—if any at all—to weather the next bushfire/plague/total societal collapse? What does my future look like? Is it secure? If I can't guarantee my physical security, shouldn't I guarantee my financial security? What about the crises we cannot yet see or imagine? It's our future and we do not know what is coming.

The flourishing of mutual aid during the pandemic put paid to the lie that if you're on welfare you're generally not contributing to society—that you couldn't possibly be a valued member of the citizenry. As people who'd lost their jobs or had them put on hold drove their elderly neighbours to doctors' appointments and organised meals for their communities, as artists held virtual concerts and readings and discussions, we got a glimpse of the type of society we could create.

Some other questions we could also be asking ourselves now: what would my life be like if I had a universal basic income? How would it change the choices I made? What would I do differently?

...

'Everyone's disposable'. 'I don't like the whole churn-and-burn mentality.' 'People think that they might be in a job for life with Qantas or the rail. But that won't happen.' 'My biggest problem is that if I lost my job tomorrow, what else would I do? I'm in my mid-fifties. When you're our age, you're considered too old, but you still need to work.' 'You are lucky if you have a job. Cost of living is so high that you just need something.' 'A lot of these big employers want to have people on casual labour, casual employment, casual conditions.' 'With a casual job they give you a tap on the shoulder, say, "There's nothing on until next Wednesday, take a few days off, we'll call you."'

These are the voices of some of the hundreds of Australians social researcher Rebecca Huntley spoke to as she travelled around the continent talking to ordinary Aussies about their lives for her book *Still Lucky*.

While Australia—with its range of benefits from paid holidays to paid sick leave to the eight-hour workday—was once seen as a workers' nirvana, this utopia is no more. Big earners have to rack up long, arduous, stressful days in order to keep their jobs; low-income workers in the casualised workforce have no idea when their next shift will be; and the unemployed on welfare are too busy fulfilling their mutual obligations to take stock and make long-term, deliberate decisions.

The casualisation of the Australian workforce has in fact long been evident—and became glaringly obvious when COVID-19 hit. As Sally McManus tells me, our economy is built upon almost one-third of the workforce in insecure work—casuals, gig workers and labour-hire contractors—all of whom come cheap. They don't have sick pay, leave entitlements, redundancy or superannuation payments.

'Every one of these workers is caught up in a cycle of trapdoor economics, where every day they go to work, they are just one bad experience away from losing their job and falling through the trapdoor into economic crisis,' she says. 'We've created an economy fuelled by anxiety and uncertainty. It's corrosive to those families and communities who have to navigate their way from pay cheque to pay cheque, not really knowing what next week has in store for them.'

Compounding growing job insecurity is the impact technological change will have on the job market. A key reason for the increased interest in a UBI is the deep-rooted belief that in numerous industries, such as taxi driving and warehouse distribution, artificial intelligence and automation will eliminate the need for human labour and thus destroy the very jobs people have worked so hard to get. In fact, a 2015 study by the Committee for Economic Development of Australia (CEDA) found that around 40 per cent of jobs in Australia are at high risk of being computerised or automated in the next ten to fifteen years.

This threat raises lots of questions. What happens when the labour market no longer provides enough jobs for everyone? Since our welfare system is based on the assumption that people are capable of achieving independence through paid work, and that welfare support is temporary, where does that leave us when the job market fails us? If the labour market is not going to cut it, isn't now the time to revolutionise the welfare system? This is not just a matter of merely weathering the change, but being ahead of the curve, and thus being able to shape it.

'In a world where technology is likely to drive either job losses, or at the very least, a rise in precarious employment, the idea that people should have to rely on having a job in order to participate in society in a decent way is an increasingly obscene idea,' Tim Dunlop writes in his book *Why the Future Is Workless*. 'To maintain our current work ethic—one that equates having a job with human decency and moral rectitude—is not only anachronistic but cruel.'

This predicament implores us to rethink our understanding of what work is. What does 'work' actually mean? How could we redefine it? What if we could learn to value unpaid work in the same way we value paid work? What benefits could that bring to us, our community, our society? What if we understood—I mean, *really* understood—that wealth is socially generated and that we, as members of the citizenry, have the right to a fair share of that wealth?

•••

The amount that Australian families pay for child care, as a proportion of household income, is among the highest in the developed world. At some point, almost every parent has had to face the difficult choice: do I send my children to child care or stay at home to the detriment of my career to look after them?

If ever there were an opportunity to expose the difficult choices women make, the hours they spend on domestic work and how little society 'pays' for this work, the pandemic has been it.

In early April 2020, the federal government announced that child care would be free. This was a reaction to mass withdrawals from child-care services by families who had been thrown into financial uncertainty or who were worried about being infected by the virus. The decision to make child care free was also essential to keeping the economy and our health-care system running—three-quarters of health-care professionals are women and almost all child carers are too. This change assumed, with good reason, that without such an intervention women would be the ones staying at home to care for their children.

As families went into lockdown and millions of couples retreated from their offices to the home, we faced a potential reckoning. Was this the moment that women had been waiting for, when men would become acutely aware of the amount of labour that goes into looking after children? It's not even just about children. What about the amount of labour that goes into running a home? Washing. Cleaning. Cooking. Caring. Was now the time to reconfigure the division of labour in the household?

It quickly became evident that this wouldn't be the revolution so many of us were waiting for. A survey for the *New York Times* found that half of male respondents believed they did most of the home schooling; three per cent of women agreed. Seventy per cent of women said they were fully or mostly responsible for housework during the lockdown—roughly the same in pre-pandemic times. It would be reasonable to expect similar findings in Australia.

'Care is something that is seen as coming naturally to women so it's not a skill that people want to pay for,' says Lyn Craig, professor of sociology and social policy at the University of Melbourne. 'Basically, it's misogyny, and it just devalues women's time and efforts.'

It has been estimated that the monetary value of unpaid care work in Australia is $650.1 billion, the equivalent of more than half of our GDP. What if we valued women's unpaid domestic work in the informal economy the way that we value paid work in the formal economy? What impact could that have on gender inequality and power dynamics?

'Our GDP leaves out all the unpaid work on which society depends,' says feminist, author and academic Eva Cox. 'It leaves out just about all the things that get dumped on women, whether we like it or not. You know, we're genetically designed according to a lot of beliefs to be good at housework and the like, and we don't even have to be paid for it because after all, if it comes naturally, we haven't had to learn it. There's no way you can seriously measure it, but it should be recognised. A UBI is a way of recognising it.'

If women stopped doing all this work, the official economy would literally grind to a halt. A UBI would acknowledge that the informal economy is what enables the formal economy to function.

The informal economy isn't just unpaid women's work in the household. There is also the unpaid work that is done outside the home, in the community, for the community, like what we saw with the flourishing of mutual-aid groups during the pandemic. Implementing a UBI could help us to recognise and revalue a whole raft of social contributions—contributions that we relied on during the bushfires, the pandemic and other crises—and which many rely on to survive day-to-day. What impact could that have on society?

'Care is such an important idea—not the care of children but care of community, care of elderly, care of country and ecosystems, and so I think a basic income could allow people the time to be able to do that,' Dr Klein says.

The mutual aid that proliferated during the pandemic, when people had time to step back, take stock and breathe deeply, should give us pause now. That moment, which has altered our lives forever, afforded us insight into the type of community, society, country we could create. We began to see what *might be*.

As Cox argues, a UBI could be transformative in that it could not just encourage a socially contributory citizenry, but it could give people an opportunity to think about what a better life could look like in that mould. She argues that a UBI could force a fundamental shift in how we view ourselves: away from being consumers, competitors and time-poor workaholics, towards being participatory members of society.

It could make visible everything that already exists but is not recognised and therefore not valued. This would create a more just, realistic way of looking at how society is already structured as well as allowing radical (and necessary) applications for the society of the future.

In his book, *Utopia for Realists: And How We Can Get There*, Rutger Bregman puts forward a poignant question, an alternative way of viewing why a UBI is essential:

> We should be posing a different question altogether: Which knowledge and skills do we want our children to have in 2030? Then, instead of anticipating and adapting, we'd be focusing on steering and creating. Instead of wondering what we need to do to make a living in this or that bullshit job, we could ponder how we want to make a living. This is a question no trend watcher can answer. How could they? They only follow the trends, they don't make them. That part is up to us.

•••

If you were to google 'Wilcannia', a remote and predominantly Aboriginal town in north-western NSW, you would be advised on tourist blogs, 'Don't stop in Wilcannia.' The town of about seven hundred, most of whom are the Barkindji people who have been living on the banks of the Darling River for the past forty thousand years, has long been described by mainstream media as a hotbed of violence, alcoholism, poverty and dysfunctional behaviour. All of these are, of course, considered 'Aboriginal problems'.

In the town, there's one small supermarket—an overly generous description of a space that offers little more than some exorbitantly priced basics—and two petrol stations, one of which has a small takeaway joint attached that sells Chiko Rolls and lollies, a hospital, a post office, two schools, a police station, a bowling club and a pub. A loaf of white bread goes for eight dollars and a slab of VB beer is upwards of seventy dollars. The nearest town is Broken Hill, more than two hours away by car.

Poverty is pervasive in Wilcannia. So are chronic diseases, skin diseases, mental-health problems, joblessness. At any given point—particularly when there is a funeral—three-bedroom homes may sleep as many as twenty people. To make ends meet, some families skip meals or have no option but to leave vegetables and fruit out of their diet.

'The people of Wilcannia need the basics: a secure roof over their heads; good food on the table; good sanitation,' says Dr Stephen Gaggin, who works for Maari Ma Health in Wilcannia.

Due to the lack of job opportunities in Wilcannia, many people rely on welfare to get by. As a condition of income support, remote-area participants—the majority of whom are Aboriginal—must engage in twenty hours of work for the dole, five days a week, as part of an initiative called the Community Development Program (CDP). The purpose of the program is to 'increase participants' skills and contribute to their community'.

In Wilcannia, this often means cleaning public toilets and parks.

If you don't turn up, you're at risk of having your payment cancelled or losing a handful of cash per day.

'If you don't go for one day, you can lose welfare support,' says Brendon Adams, community leader and Wilcannia River Radio station manager. 'It's like rations back in the thirties when they'd take your bread away. Instead, today, they take money away.'

A recent review of the CDP found that Aboriginal participants were three times more likely to be penalised for non-attendance and were penalised more often than white participants. They went without income for longer periods and were less likely to be exempted on medical grounds, despite the much higher burden of disease in Aboriginal and Torres Strait Islander communities.

More than that, as Adams tells me, the program doesn't enable the Barkindji people to participate in the cultural activities that are central to their identity and connection to the land. 'Our cultural way of living and surviving, such as fishing and going hunting for emu eggs, the government has taken away from us because they stopped the river from flowing because of the cotton farms.'

Dr Tjanara Goreng Goreng, research scholar at the Centre for Aboriginal Economic Policy Research at ANU, writes for the Green Institute, 'What kind of society are we creating where we shame people for not being able to gain employment in areas where there is virtually no available employment, or for not having the educational qualifications to work in the only jobs available?'

She argues that a universal basic income 'would provide something quite different, something socially supportive and economically viable to Indigenous communities where paid work, entrepreneurship, business and strategic investment are non-existent. It would enable individuals and families to support themselves and each other and provide for the necessities of living which welfare dependency does not.'

It is hard to underestimate what impact a UBI could have on a community like Wilcannia, and other Aboriginal and Torres Strait Islander communities. It could reduce chronic disease and other health conditions; improve nutrition; reduce alcohol and drug dependence; increase school attendance; decrease mental-health illnesses; improve living standards; improve family relationships; reduce domestic violence. The list goes on.

Strikingly, some of the benefits a UBI could bring to Wilcannia are exactly the same as those brought to the most socio-economically disadvantaged people in India. The link, perhaps difficult to make earlier, should make us open our eyes.

'A [UBI] doesn't pay back what has been taken from our First Nations people, but it is sort of a record—I wouldn't say it's a reparation, it's a way of acknowledging and providing the space to have the conversation about truth telling,' Dr Klein says. 'It's a financial transaction because a lot of First Nations people in this country are disproportionately in poverty.'

A UBI could also be seen as a vital support mechanism to correct the decades of intergenerational trauma that have been inflicted upon Indigenous communities, and that have affected every single aspect of life, including engagement with the education system and work. In partnership with adequate social programs, a UBI could lay the groundwork for healing and recovery. More than that, a UBI could provide the support, stability and security to enable Indigenous communities to remain connected to their identity, culture and the land. By freeing people of the work-for-the-dole programs, and again with adequate investment, volunteer community programs could flourish.

A UBI is not a cure-all for a community like Wilcannia, but it could provide hope for a better future.

'Parents have no jobs; they're depressed and frustrated, and a lot are dependent on alcohol and drugs. What's the next generation got to look forward to? They've got nothing to look forward to,' Adams says. 'So, what's going to happen? They're going to move to the city and lose their identity. When they're forced into the city without any skills, anything can happen, from depression to suicide to even selling yourself. These worst-case scenarios are real.'

Adams knows. He's lived it. He was a street kid and lived rough in a cardboard box on the streets of Brisbane and Sydney.

'I know what it's like to have nothing. To have no identity. To be classed as nothing.'

•••

So, what does a UBI cost and how could we go about implementing it?

There are various amounts scholars have put forward as the 'right' amount. Economist and professor at the University of Queensland John Quiggin estimates the cost of a fully implemented UBI to be between 5 and 10 per cent of GDP, depending on the size of the payment. Australia's United Workers Union has called for a UBI that's equal to the minimum wage of $740 a week, which comes very close to the $1500 fortnightly wage subsidy program, JobKeeper. Whatever the amount, a UBI that is adequate must be set at a level high enough to protect citizens against poverty. It must also be flexible enough to be increased in line with consumer prices or the real value will depreciate over time in comparison with inflation.

As Tim Dunlop writes in *The Future of Everything*, 'Proponents should be careful not to get too bogged down in the minutiae of costings and implementation (as important as they will ultimately be) and thus reduce it to yet another technocratic debate.' Like Dunlop, I'm not going to get into mathematical modelling or the nitty-gritty, but to institute a UBI would require a dramatic rethink of taxation and spending—something that the pandemic has illustrated is possible. In a nutshell, it would require a higher degree of taxation of the rich to pay for it.

Jeremy Baskin argues that a UBI would be run through the Australian Taxation Office rather than Centrelink, and that the money would be taxable income, so the tax office would recoup a significant proportion from higher earners.

In the book *Implementing a Basic Income in Australia: Pathways Forward*, which brings together Australian experts from different fields, Quiggin suggests that one way of making implementation possible is to start with 'basic' rather than 'universal': 'That is, begin by providing sufficient income to support a decent standard of living to those most in need, then expand it to the entire population,' he writes.

Another implementation path is what political economists Troy Henderson from the University of Sydney and Ben Spies-Butcher from Macquarie University term the 'stepping-stone approach'. It would involve two initial stages: redesigning Australia's pension system to make it genuinely universal by removing means testing, and then introducing a new youth allowance, a youth basic income. Once these two are in place, the path to a fully functioning UBI is achieved as increasingly large sections of society are covered by one of the two universal and unconditional payments until we eventually meet in the middle and cover everyone.

Their model is not simply about economics; it's about politics. As Tim Hollo from the Green Institute argues, slowly enabling more people to access their fair share of society's wealth has the immediate effect of reversing the stigma associated with welfare into something that people demand, something that people want. By doing so, we can garner support for reconceiving Australia's approach to social security and inequality.

If we did take a 'basic' or 'stepping-stone' approach to a UBI, it would have to simultaneously reach enough people and be generous enough to have an impact. Rolling out a trial or taking one of the two approaches above would be pointless if the amount were just a few thousand dollars a year.

With a policy that is based on the principles of universality and unconditionality, it is somewhat difficult to run trials—it's almost as if an all-in approach is needed (at least in my opinion). Given that a UBI is about us, the people, and that all wealth is socially generated, meaning that it is part of the 'commons', I am inclined to argue that we could use a deliberative, democratic process to bring about a UBI. After all, a chief executive officer cannot do their job if their shirts are not pressed by the drycleaner and their child is not looked after at school; the waiter cannot get to work if the bus driver is not driving; the lifeguard is out of a job if the pool has to close because the chlorine company has folded.

If we believe that a UBI could be an important part of making our society more democratic, more inclusive, more equal, then it only makes sense that we bring it about in a democratic, deliberative way. We could use citizens' juries or assemblies or a People's Chamber—as discussed in chapter one—to do so. We could harness digital technology to conduct citizen polls to test recommendations for how a UBI could be financed and implemented. Taking deliberative democratic action to implement a democratising project, we have the ability to radically reconceive the relationship between citizen and state, to reconceive the notion of power, and to reconceive our idea of what it means to be part of the citizenry—whether that is from the perspective of the government or the citizen.

We can look to the Melbourne Dance Company for inspiration. Recognising the poor working conditions of Australia's artists, it proposes a radically different interpretation of the dance 'company' model. The MDC proposes a unique company structure that distributes 90 per cent of its $10 million budget to 225 company members in the form of a $30,000 living wage. In addition, each member is allocated $10,000 towards their annual artistic project. The remainder of the money is dedicated to running the company—administration, payroll, fundraising.

The core ambition of the MDC model is the fair distribution of taxpayers' money to artists to pay for their work. In doing so, it acknowledges not only the sense of community that is at the core of dance, but also encourages greater diversity in who can practise (not just those with wealthy parents) and puts a monetary value on the work of artists. It gives artists what is rightfully theirs.

In whatever way a UBI could come about, what the pandemic has illustrated is that change is possible. Big policy changes are, in fact, possible overnight. We now realise that the basis of our social order is not rigid and inevitable but rather mouldable and malleable.

'As the emergency measures have shown, there is no fundamental obstacle to doing this,' Quiggin says. 'The budget cost would be substantially less than that of the current measures and could be financed by forgoing tax cuts scheduled for coming years.

'The question is whether we try to return to the failed policies of the past.'

• • •

We're part of a system that encourages us to work more in order to earn money to buy more things that we don't need. And then we're told that the shiny new things we bought aren't shiny or new enough and that we need an upgrade. And so it goes.

Simon Lewis and Mark Maslin, authors of the *The Human Planet: How We Created the Anthropocene*, argue that a UBI could break the link between work and consumption. 'Consumption is the payback for being ever-more productive at work. Indeed, it makes little sense to curb consumption when we know we will have to be ever-more productive at work regardless of our choices,' they write in the *Guardian*.

> UBI reduces dependency, giving people the agency to say no to undesirable work, and yes to opportunities that often lie out of reach. With UBI we could all think long-term, well beyond the next payday. We could care for ourselves, others, and the wider world, as living in the Anthropocene demands.

Similarly, Naomi Klein argues in her book *This Changes Everything: Capitalism vs. the Climate* that a new economic order is needed in the face of the climate crisis. '[I]t is counterproductive to force people to work in jobs that simply fuel unsustainable consumption,' she writes.

If we break the link between work and consumption, we could dramatically reduce the harm we are inflicting on the planet by slowing down the drudgery of producing and consuming things that we don't need or know that we even want.

We could work less, consume less and still be happy.

More than that, a UBI could also give us the opportunity to free ourselves from work that is environmentally damaging, such as that undertaken in the fossil-fuel industry. Many people who fear climate change work in these industries, alongside climate-change deniers. Why do they do it? To change things from the inside? Because of resignation that things will never change? Because mining is the only job in the town? In this sense, a UBI could shift behaviours, choices and attitudes in some of industries we talk about less frequently in the context of a UBI from fossil-fuel workers to farmers to accountants.

'If we're trying to do things for the environment, a UBI would be very useful for that,' Cox tells me. 'I don't think people value that. So really, what it's saying is that we value the unpaid contributions you make, and we value you for making them. Also, if we're serious about not fucking up the environment by digging more stuff out of it, you know, and spending more on energy, this might be a way.'

One of the greatest lessons to come from the pandemic is that SARS-CoV-2 is more than a virus. It is a symptom of the ailing health of our planet. It symbolises our destructive relationship with nature and signals—if we needed any more evidence—that we are in the midst of a climate emergency and are facing an ecological crisis.

This is not an isolated event, and that is why it is so critical we do not view a vaccine against this deadly, frightening virus as a panacea to our problems. *If* an effective vaccine does arrive, we cannot become complacent. This is a moment of reckoning, and we must use it to create a more equal, fair, just, democratic society for all of us. One way to do that would be to introduce a universal basic income. Something for all of us, by us. Something that recognises that we, as part of the commons, are all entitled to a certain standard of living, a certain freedom of choice and, most importantly, dignity.

Moreover, this crisis has shown us that the most important work we do is the care we provide to one another. Care that is not recognised in the economy nor reflected in our pay cheques. Without that care, without that love, without that support, where would we be today?

In *The White Plague: Tuberculosis, Man and Society*, Jean-Baptiste and René Jules Dubos describe tuberculosis as 'the first penalty that capitalistic society had to pay for the ruthless exploitation of labour'. How will COVID-19 and its aftermath be remembered?

3 | INDIGENOUS AFFAIRS

> 'The microbe is nothing; the terrain, everything.'
>
> LOUIS PASTEUR

Elder Cyril Hunter sits by the edge of the Darling River, an emu egg resting elegantly in his lap like a baby. He holds up the navy, thick-shelled egg, its weight obvious as he clasps it with both hands.

'You know, this will feed the lot of us,' he says.

The river is flowing—albeit slowly—behind him for the first time in three years. Its murky waters are the soul of the people; the holder of rich culture, stories and history of thousands of years, threatened with evaporation.

The scene around us is serene: the reddened earth, trees swaying in the autumn wind, gumnuts falling onto our shoes, flies swarming our faces. We feel safe and far removed from the world-altering event unfolding outside our confines: the COVID-19 pandemic.

In the local Barkindji language, the Aboriginal people of Wilcannia are 'people of the river'; 'Barka' means river.

'I fought for this land,' Elder Cyril says. 'The river used to be so beautiful, it did. I fought for this land for more than thirty years. I grew up in a tin hut along the river.'

In 2015, the Barkindji people were recognised as the traditional owners of the land in far western NSW, after a successful court ruling on the state's largest native title claim. They were recognised eighteen years after the claim was first lodged.

It was the sixth native title determination in NSW and the largest—covering 128,000 square kilometres—from Wentworth, at the Victorian border, to near Wanaaring, in the state's north-west, including Wilcannia and Broken Hill. But while native title recognises their rights to the land, it does not include rights over the water.

For the Barkindji people, a healthy river is everything. For Elder Cyril and the others by the river bank, the flowing water is a source of nourishment, both literally and metaphorically.

In late 2018, an estimated one million native fish turned up dead in the Darling River and Menindee Lakes. Images of dead fish floated up onto our television screens while we celebrated Christmas. It was difficult to watch, just as it was difficult to watch televised images of burnt koalas and kangaroos during our Black Summer. But it was more difficult to turn away.

Reading the figure *one million* is one thing; seeing it is another. The three major species of fish killed included hundreds of thousands of small bony bream, Murray cod, which have an estimated lifespan of up to 114 years, and silver perch, which can live for two decades. While the cause of the disaster was a combination of drought (not unprecedented) and over-extraction for upstream irrigation (predominantly by cotton farms), it was the direct result of government mismanagement of the Murray–Darling river system. For years the river had been dying; for years the government had been mismanaging the Barwon–Darling system and irrigators.

'When they take the water from a Barkindji person, they take our blood. They're killing us,' Barkindji Elder and artist Badger Bates wrote in the *Guardian*. 'It's not just Barkindji people who are feeling it. It's the white people and other people too.

'How can I teach culture when they're taking our beloved Barka away? There's nothing to teach if there's no river. The river is everything. It's my life, my culture. You take the water from us; we've got nothing.'

For the children of Wilcannia and elsewhere, the stories of the river told by their parents, grandparents and Elders had become something they could only dream about, something etched into their imaginations as they lay next to their brothers and sisters at nightfall.

'Oh, the Darling River. We are the people of the river. The Barkindji people of the river. The river is our home,' the children of Wilcannia chant.

Cyril Hunter moves towards the edge of the river, a thin fishing rod in hand. His teenage grandson, Jai, is out catching yabbies, bream and cod for first time in years. Cyril bought him a canoe to glide up and down the river—something that he enjoys too, while it is still possible to do so. Just a few months later, when some of the Wilcannia mob call me, they tell me the river has withered away again into almost nothing. It is no surprise that over the past few years the phrase 'the Barka's burka' ('the Darling River is dead') has grown in popularity.

It is late April 2020 when I meet Elder Cyril. At the time we think Australia is facing the height of the pandemic. Time soon reveals that what we thought to be true was not—just like so many other things this pandemic is teaching us.

Two months ago, the seventy-three-year-old moved his family down here, to set up camp on the riverbank as protection from the novel coronavirus. With memories of past plagues like the swine flu of 2009 still fresh, the threat of a new, deadly virus was more than enough for him to take swift action—action that could save their lives.

The campsite meshes the old with the new. Modern appliances support traditional ways of life: a generator underneath a tree illuminates the kitchen at night as the mob cook kangaroo tail and boil emu eggs.

'You can see for yourself what we're doing here. We have everything we need,' Elder Cyril says.

Their action speaks to the argument of integration over assimilation and the need for a bicultural future of 'people who grow socially and economically strong without losing their languages and cultures', as Noel Pearson writes in his Quarterly Essay *A Rightful Place*. 'In Australia, [I]ndigenous peoples have not been allowed to make their own choices about how to reconcile their cultures with the demands of development.'

The Hunters' campsite comprises four tents, an open firepit and an open kitchen. Several chairs for fishing and storytelling sit along the riverbank. They are intentionally stationed a few metres apart from one another. Upon arrival at the campsite, you must first wash your hands. Physical distancing and hand hygiene are two of the best defences against this deadly disease.

'Coronavirus would wipe us out,' Elder Cyril says. 'It's very sad for the people here.'

...

One of the greatest tragedies to ever befall humanity was the influenza pandemic of 1918–19. Also known as the Spanish flu, the virus spread with bewildering speed around the world, overwhelming India, reaching Australia and even the remote Pacific islands.

In just eighteen months, at least a third of the world's population was infected. Estimates vary widely on the number of people who perished, from one million to 100 million. If the upper estimates are correct, the Spanish flu killed more people than both World Wars combined. It rivalled the Black Death of the fourteenth century for mortality, and social and economic impact.

The disease arrived on Australia's shores in January 1919. About a third of the population was infected and some 15,000 people died. We don't know how many Aboriginal and Torres Strait Islander people lost their lives—they weren't counted in the country's official statistics. What we do know is that it completely destroyed communities.

Ninety years later, in 2009, the swine flu pandemic, caused by the H1N1 virus, hit communities around the world. It became the second H1N1 influenza virus to cause a pandemic, after the devastating events of 1918–19. Swine flu infection rates vary from 700 million to up to 1.4 billion people: between 11 per cent and 21 per cent of the global population was infected. While the number of deaths reported to the WHO was just under 20,000, it's estimated that almost 300,000 died from swine flu. It proved to be no deadlier than the yearly seasonal flu, but as with all diseases, it was deadlier for certain groups of people.

When the H1N1 virus arrived in Australia in 2009, it took a disproportionately heavy toll on Indigenous people, who ultimately suffered a death rate around six times higher than the general population. The virus's first victim was a twenty-six-year-old Aboriginal man from the Western Australian Aboriginal community of Kiwirrkurra. Located in the Gibson Desert, it's the most remote community in Australia. It is eight hundred kilometres west of Alice Springs. The young man died in Royal Adelaide Hospital on 19 June 2009.

Aboriginal and Torres Strait Islander people made up 2.5 per cent of the population at the time of the swine flu pandemic. However, they accounted for 11 per cent of the 37,683 cases recorded across the country. They also accounted for 16 per cent of the hospitalisations and nearly 10 per cent of admissions to intensive care units.

The alarming infection rate begged the question: what are the precise mechanisms by which this disease (and others, like trachoma and rheumatic heart disease) afflict some bodies more than others?

So, when word of a new virus began to circulate in early 2020, James Ward, a leading Indigenous public-health expert based at the University of Queensland's Poche Centre for Indigenous Health, knew that to avert another catastrophe Australia's response would have to be drastically different. It would have to be swift and closely involve the communities.

'The biggest lesson we learnt from 2009 was that the response was late,' he says. 'We were far too late to mount a response and there was no involvement of Aboriginal people. Aboriginal people weren't involved in the discussion around preparedness and response to the pandemic.'

In the face of decades of poor policy, government neglect and a lack of funding, the Aboriginal community-controlled health sector sprang into action, creating a unique infectious-disease response to the virus. It was the first time in Australia's history that a health response was tailored to a specific group of people, by that specific group of people.

There was no other option. Doctors across the country were warning that, without swift intervention, whole communities could be wiped out by this novel coronavirus. 'We had to make sure that we discussed and tackled all possible scenarios, situations that might arise,' Professor Ward says.

In early April 2020, I speak with Dr Jason King, a primary health-care physician working in Yarrabah. Yarrabah, considered one of Australia's most disadvantaged communities, is located in Far North Queensland. One of the most disadvantaged, but by no means the most isolated: Yarrabah is just a forty-five-minute drive from Cairns, the gateway to the one of the world's most stunning natural wonders, the Great Barrier Reef.

He speaks with urgency. I can feel his anxiety down the phone. He rattles off statistics about the Yarrabah community, 90 per cent of whom are Aboriginal and Torres Strait Islanders.

There are 3500 people in the town, but only 350 homes. Some houses have up to twenty people living in them. They are not all connected to the power grid. Some have poor access to running water. Around 850 people are over the age of fifty, 80 per cent of whom have a chronic disease. More than eighty people are over the age of seventy. The community has the highest rate of rheumatic heart disease in the world.

'I get cold sweats thinking what this would all mean for Yarrabah,' Dr King tells me. 'Overcrowding tells this story straightaway.'

Very early on in our fight against the virus, we knew that our two best defences were physical distancing and hand-washing—simple interventions that in some communities across the continent are simply impossible. As prominent doctor and medical anthropologist Paul Farmer writes in his book *Infections and Inequalities*, 'Social inequalities shape not only the distribution of emerging diseases but also the health outcomes of the those afflicted—a fact that is often downplayed.'

The Aboriginal community-controlled health sector knew this. Time was not on their side. Across the country they ensured that clear health messages reached communities in their own languages. The Northern Land Council translated health messages into eighteen different languages for the Top End and posted them as videos on social media. The faces in all the videos were Indigenous. The Apunipima Cape York Health Council collaborated with First Nations contacts in Canada, sharing templates of their communities' pandemic plans. As early as January 2020, the Kimberley Aboriginal Medical Services had ordered personal protective equipment.

Some remote communities, without any word from the government, quietly shut their borders. First it was the A<u>n</u>angu Pitjantjatjara Yankunytjatjara Lands in remote South Australia, followed by some Cape York communities in Far North Queensland, including Yarrabah. In doing so, these communities exercised sovereignty that they had rarely commanded but never ceded.

The federal government, meanwhile, set up a national Aboriginal and Torres Strait Islander Advisory Group on COVID-19 to fast-track an emergency response plan for Aboriginal communities. The group—which Ward advises—is made up of leaders from the Aboriginal community-controlled health sector, state and territory health and medical officials, Aboriginal communicable disease experts, the Australian Indigenous Doctors' Association, and the National Indigenous Australians Agency. Among the principles on which the group works are shared decision-making, power-sharing, self-determination and empowerment.

By the time the federal government announced travel restrictions into Indigenous areas on 26 March, local efforts to protect communities had been underway for weeks, if not months. When Prime Minister Scott Morrison addressed the nation around the same time, he recommended that anyone over the age of seventy go into self-isolation. For non-Indigenous Australians with pre-existing health problems, it was anyone over sixty; for Indigenous people, it was anyone over fifty. It was a shocking admission of the failure of successive governments to improve the health of our Indigenous people.

But the prime minister neglected to explain why. Why should Indigenous Australians with pre-existing conditions need to self-isolate from fifty while non-Indigenous Australians with the same conditions have to self-isolate from sixty? How could this ten-year disparity be acceptable?

By this time, many Indigenous Australians living in cities had returned to their native lands to isolate. Others, like Cyril Hunter and his family, had opted to camp out in the bush to protect themselves and ease some of the burden on their overcrowded homes. In other remote communities, outstations were set up specifically for the Elders. At the time of writing, in mid-2020, many remain locked down in their own way, doing what needs to be done to 'shield themselves from a mainstream Australia even more fatal to black lives than usual', says acclaimed Aboriginal writer of Goorie and European heritage Melissa Lucashenko.

Pat Turner, of Gudanji-Arrernte heritage, is the chief executive officer of the National Aboriginal Community Controlled Health

Organisation (NACCHO), the national authority on Aboriginal and Torres Strait Islander primary care, which brings together 143 Aboriginal community-controlled health services across the country. These primary health-care services are initiated and operated by the local Aboriginal community to deliver holistic, comprehensive and culturally appropriate health care to the community that controls it.

Turner works with people across the entire country and her fear was palpable. 'We were particularly worried that if COVID-19 got into a discrete Aboriginal community, whether it was Cherbourg or Yarrabah or the Kimberley, that it would be devastating,' she says. 'I knew that a pandemic would be extremely damaging to our people who are the most vulnerable. One of our priorities was the protection of our older people, who are holders of our knowledge and teachers to the younger generations about cultural heritage, language, the country, medicine, everything. They are like our university professors. We could not afford to lose them to COVID-19.'

Turner wasn't just losing sleep over remote communities. She was afraid of what the virus would mean to the majority of Aboriginal and Torres Strait Islander people who live in urban areas. Systemic racism. Overcrowding. Poverty. Low socio-economic status. All the things that facilitate the rapid spread of disease. And what about the homeless? Those who have no roof over their heads, who have limited access to sanitation? And what about the Aboriginal and Torres Strait Islander people—who are, proportionally, the most incarcerated people on the planet—locked up in prisons? What would happen if COVID-19 spread throughout the prison system? Would the government take action?

In an article for the *Saturday Paper*, Darumbal/South Sea Islander journalist Amy McQuire writes:

> There is a common narrative about Indigenous health, based on dysfunction and vulnerability, in which Aboriginal people themselves are blamed through the mantra of individual choices. There is little room to focus on strength and agency when you are simply a 'problem' to be solved, a 'gap' to be filled. The Aboriginal health sector's response to COVID-19 has flipped that on its head.

It has indeed. At the time of writing, since the virus arrived in Australia in late January 2020, there has not been a single COVID-19 case in any rural or remote Indigenous community. Very few Indigenous people living in urban and regional centres have been infected. None have lost their lives. What the Aboriginal community-controlled health sector has done with the funding of an 'oily rag'—as Pat Turner says—is nothing short of a miracle.

'No one is better placed to solve the issues that confront us,' writes Noel Pearson in *A Rightful Place*. 'Until Indigenous Australians are allowed to take responsibility for our own lives, development and equality will not be achieved.'

Very simply, as everyone I spoke with highlighted, the Aboriginal community-controlled health sector has been so successful against the pandemic because the response has been led by communities, by the very people who know the solutions to their problems.

'Have a look at the way the Aboriginal community-controlled health organisations responded to the pandemic and the record they have up to this point,' says Torres Strait Islander author Thomas Mayor. 'What that is is effectively a demonstration of how well a Voice to Parliament will work. It's a demonstration of how the Uluru

Statement from the Heart would work at a much greater level on many other issues.'

CLOSING THE DIVIDE

'Unprecedented' has become one of those hackneyed words to describe this seismic moment. Yet the presence of a deadly new disease is not unprecedented for Aboriginal and Torres Strait Islander peoples. Nor the 'enforced social measures that fragment how we interact, and who with. Not the laying to waste of the environment. Not the strategies of triage, and stratified disposability of human lives,' as Gomeroi poet and essayist Alison Whittaker writes in the *Guardian*.

The pandemic is preceded by events horrific, tragic and violent for Indigenous Australians. And precedents set by successive governments have left Indigenous Australians incredibly vulnerable—not only to contracting the virus but succumbing to it. What the pandemic has done is expose Australia's appalling inability to improve Indigenous health outcomes.

'COVID-19 has enabled us to hold a mirror up to Australia's population and say, "Past policies have failed this population group,"' says Justin Files, executive manager of social and community programs at Maari Ma Health, an Aboriginal community-controlled health organisation in far western NSW.

In 2007, the federal government launched the Close the Gap campaign, which aims to bring the health and life expectancy of Indigenous Australians up to parity with non-Indigenous Australians within a generation. It is not working. The 2020 Close the Gap report found that the target to close the life expectancy gap by 2031 was not on track. It also found that the gap between Indigenous and non-Indigenous child mortality had actually widened. At 141 per

100,000, it is twice that of non-Indigenous children. In fact, the report found that only two targets were being met: early education and Year 12 attainment.

A major target—which itself is another campaign, Close the Gap for Vision—has been to eliminate trachoma. Australia remains the only country in the developed world to have endemic levels of trachoma, the leading preventable cause of blindness around the world. In 2018, Nepal, one of the poorest countries on the planet, eliminated trachoma. It is 100 per cent preventable and 100 per cent irreversible. The disease disappeared from most of Australia more than a century ago, but persists in remote Aboriginal communities which still lack safe washing facilities, and which have poor and chronically overcrowded housing.

'It is our national shame,' says Hugh Taylor, the Harold Mitchell Professor of Indigenous Eye Health at the University of Melbourne. He has been working on eye health for more than forty years. 'It is the result of atrocious living conditions. It is embarrassing.'

Trachoma predominantly infects young children and is the result of having a dirty face, of not washing snot and dried tears away. The disease is so contagious that when children are infected once, they are likely to be reinfected dozens of times. The condition not only hampers their health, but their ability to learn. In remote communities where families simply do not have the means to keep their children's faces clean, what incentive is there for children to complete school? What future do they have to look forward to? For a wealthy country like Australia, which ostensibly values the 'fair go', these questions are crushing, the answers shattering.

'In Nepal, in Tanzania, parents know that if their child finishes school and gets an education, that is their way out,' Professor Taylor says. 'There is no incentive for Aboriginal children. So, kids finish school and then what? What do they do? What do they have to look forward to? The only other place where I have seen such a level of disempowerment is in refugee camps where refugees have nowhere to go.

'Our Aboriginal communities have had power stripped from them. We must put them at the centre of the response. We need the Uluru Statement from the Heart.'

For the past fourteen years, the Close the Gap campaign's targets have been the prism through which we examine Indigenous 'disadvantage'. Governments are obsessed with targets. The adoption of targets and the tyranny of metrics has not served us well. After all, targets do not drive change. They simply measure how well an issue is being addressed, in this case through the application of government resources.

In *A Rightful Place*, Noel Pearson describes how misguided it is to 'reduce the Indigenous predicament in Australia to the banal idea of "Closing the Gap" on Indigenous disadvantage'.

He writes: 'There is something more fundamental at stake: whether the Yolngu of Arnhem Land will find a place in the Australian nation so that—honouring their fathers and mothers, as obliged by the Second Commandment—they may live long on the earth.'

At the end of July 2020, as Australia continued to record skyrocketing COVID-19 cases, the prime minister and Ken Wyatt, the minister for Indigenous Australians, addressed the media to unveil the new national agreement on Closing the Gap.

It was the culmination of months of negotiation between the Coalition of Peaks and state and territory governments. The Coalition of Peaks is an alliance of more than fifty Aboriginal and Torres Strait Islander community-controlled peak organisations, which represent thousands of Aboriginal and Islander groups concerned with health, housing, education, justice and culture. What emerged from the negotiation were four new priority reforms and sixteen socioeconomic targets committing federal, state and territory governments to working in partnership with Aboriginal organisations to design and deliver on priority areas such as justice reform, housing and suicide.

New targets for 2031 include: 88 per cent of Aboriginal families not living in overcrowded homes; moving 30 per cent of young Indigenous prisoners out of detention (something which could have been immediately addressed had the federal Council of Attorneys-General decided to raise the age of criminal responsibility from ten to fourteen years); reducing adult incarceration by 15 per cent; 70 per cent of young Indigenous people to hold a tertiary qualification; and reducing by 45 per cent the number of Indigenous children in out-of-home care.

A key difference in the new agreement is that, for the first time, Indigenous people shared decision-making with governments. They had direct involvement in negotiating the targets and will assist in implementing the agreement. Addressing the media, Scott Morrison conceded, 'We told Indigenous Australians what the gap was that we were going to close. And somehow thought they should be thankful for that.' The concession carried a clause: the agreement 'isn't about buckets of money'—an interesting revelation, given that the peak bodies that will be doing the on-the-ground work rely on government funding in order to operate.

Turner, who is lead convener of the Coalition of Peaks and co-chair of the joint council on Closing the Gap, is focused on four priority reform areas that she believes will actually 'make the difference': the empowerment of Aboriginal and Torres Strait Islander people through shared decision-making; the delivery of high-quality services by building the community-controlled sector; making governments and their organisations and institutions accountable for Closing the Gap by improving mainstream institutions; and Indigenous data sovereignty, which enables communities to have access to, and use of, locally derived and relevant data and information to drive their own development.

'The community really aren't bothered about targets; they want structural reform,' Turner says. 'What's needed is for Aboriginal and Torres Strait Islander people to be party to the determination of priorities, of best program responses...instead of governments sitting in their ivory towers around the country dreaming up what is good for Aboriginals. It's proven that approach is not viable or sustainable. It's at the whim of politics and can change at every election.'

The last priority reform area was something that came about during the Coalition of Peaks' countrywide community engagement process. It was born out of frustration that the Indigenous data environment is a paradox: while an enormous body of data about Indigenous Australians has been collected, it is not useful to them or really to anybody else. Little or no data for them and by them exists.

The easiest way to demonstrate this to type 'Indigenous Australians' into Google, which quickly pulls up a range of grim statistics related to their health and socio-economic status. Overcrowded homes. High rates of diabetes. High numbers on welfare support. Poor school performance. High rates of incarceration.

It is something that Palawa woman Maggie Walter, professor of sociology at the University of Tasmania, terms '5D data': data that focus on Difference, Disparity, Disadvantage, Dysfunction and Deprivation. 'In the portrait of Australia created by current Indigenous data, Aboriginal and Torres Strait Islander people are missing—except as a problem,' she writes in her *Griffith Review* essay 'The Voice of Indigenous Data'. 'And this is how most non-Indigenous people, including the political class and policymakers, know us.'

The consequence of this cannot be overstated. Depicting Indigenous Australians through the prism of 5D data has led us to believe that Indigenous Australians are a problem to be fixed by white people, who can save them.

Even more devastating, as Walter describes, is that this data has also informed how Indigenous people have come to understand themselves and their place in society. What effect would it have on your psyche to grow up being told that your people are sick, that they die young, that they are in prison, that they don't finish school, that they are on welfare so there is no point finishing school anyway, that your friend committed suicide, and that your mother's friend's son went to prison for stealing a candy bar?

Another fundamental flaw of 5D data, as Walter highlights, is the individualised focus on the person or the family. For example, what is the point of collecting data on Aboriginal children's school attendance if data is not also collected on the school and its resources? How well does the school support the needs of Aboriginal kids? How supportive is the environment? What about the child's home environment? Is it conducive to learning?

Indigenous data sovereignty, as Walter writes, is 'the right to determine the means of collection, access, analysis, interpretation, management, dissemination and reuse of data pertaining to the Indigenous peoples from whom they have been derived, or to whom they relate'. By rejecting the 5D data paradigm, Indigenous data sovereignty instead focuses on data that is useful—data that is about 'peoples, territories, lifeways and natural resources'. It is data that reflects their priorities, values, culture and diversity.

But while the excitement around the new agreement is palpable, there is enormous trepidation from Indigenous communities around the country who wonder if this is yet another tokenistic gesture that will have little to no benefit for the people who live this reality. And while this process and this new agreement has been vaunted by the government as 'self-determination', in practice it is not.

Professor Megan Davis, Cobble Cobble woman and pro vice-chancellor and professor of law at UNSW, reminds us that while Aboriginal peak organisations are fearless in their pursuit of equality for Aboriginal people and their access to services, they are contracted service providers. 'The peaks rely on government funds to run their organisations and these monies are pegged to the governments' outcomes, not ours,' she writes in the *Sydney Morning Herald*.

> Government can defund service deliveries and dismiss them with a wave of a pen or defund them when it so chooses…The peaks treat the symptoms, but a protected Voice in the constitution is about treating the causes of illness, of incarceration, of early death, unemployment and poor education outcomes.

The cause is structural, the result of, as the Uluru Statement describes, generations of 'the torment of our powerlessness'. We should be asking *why* Indigenous children are seventeen times more likely to be imprisoned than non-Indigenous youth; *why* trachoma persists in remote Indigenous communities while other Australians are spared; *why* Indigenous people die almost ten years earlier than non-Indigenous Australians. The gap is, fundamentally, the inability to determine one's present and future. We must ask: *why* does the gap exist in the first place?

A FIRST NATIONS VOICE

The constitution is the rule book for the federal nation of Australia. But it contains no reference to Aboriginal and Torres Strait Islander peoples' historical and present place in the country.

Under section 51 (xxvi) of the constitution, federal parliament has the power to make laws specifically about Aboriginal and Torres Strait Islander peoples. This 'race power' applies to people of all different races, but has only ever been used to pass special laws for Indigenous peoples.

In late 2015, the Referendum Council—appointed by then prime minister Malcolm Turnbull and then opposition leader Bill Shorten—was given the long-overdue task of asking Aboriginal and Torres Strait Islander peoples what form of constitutional reform they could support. Throughout 2016 and 2017 the Referendum Council held twelve regional dialogues across the country with more than a thousand Aboriginal and Torres Strait Islander peoples. These meetings considered five possible constitutional amendments to recognise Indigenous Australians.

From these deliberations, clear consensus emerged around the need for a single form of constitutional recognition: an Indigenous advisory body that would have a say in laws and policies made about Indigenous peoples. A First Nations voice.

In May 2017, 250 Aboriginal and Torres Strait Islander delegates from across the continent gathered at Uluru, a scared place home to the Aṉangu people, its traditional cultural guardians, for the First Nations National Constitutional Convention. It was here that the Uluru Statement from the Heart was born.

The statement not only calls for a First Nations Voice to be enshrined in the Australian Constitution, but also the establishment of a Makarrata Commission to 'supervise agreement-making and truth-telling between governments and Aboriginal and Torres Strait Islander people', according to the statement's information booklet.

On the final morning of the convention, Professor Megan Davis stood on the podium, with Uluru in the background, and read the Uluru Statement for the very first time. It was endorsed with a standing ovation and tears of joy.

The statement is a stark—and necessary—reminder that the first sovereign nations of the Australian continent and its adjacent islands have never ceded sovereignty. In denouncing the scale of the crisis—from incarceration to child removal to suicide—the statement is not asking for empathy; it is envisioning, and creating, a new path forward.

The Uluru Statement asks for a constitutionally guaranteed voice. The constitutional guarantee is crucial, Thomas Mayor tells me, because Indigenous bodies in the past have been set up in legislation only to be struck down in the political churn and burn. The most glaring example of this is the Aboriginal and Torres Strait Islander Commission (ATSIC). Established by the Bob Hawke Labor government in response to calls for political representation, it was immediately defunded when Liberal John Howard took office. It was completely shut down in 2005.

'The Uluru Statement is not going away because it's written to the Australian people, not to the parliament to say no,' says Mayor.

He travelled around Australia for eighteen months with the Uluru Statement canvas in his hands to raise awareness and garner support for the cause. 'But what is important is that the only way it's going to be imminent, the only way it's going to be successful, is if we can convince enough Australians to force politicians to put it to the people. That is the work ahead of us.'

The constitution can only be changed by the Australian people, in a referendum. Details of the changes would have to be agreed on by parliament before being presented to the people for a vote, and the specific details of the Voice would be legislated after the referendum. Legislation would set up the details, function, powers and processes of the Voice, according to the University of Melbourne's law school.

It has been suggested that the First Nations Voice have members who are chosen by First Nations themselves, representing local communities. These chosen members will represent the people and be accountable to the people: not to any corporation, not to any institution, not to anyone else.

And contrary to spin by right-wing media and politicians like Peter Dutton, enshrining a First Nations Voice in the constitution is not the equivalent of establishing a third chamber of parliament. As its proponents continually have to reiterate: a First Nations Voice would have no power to initiate, pass or reject bills. It would have no veto powers. The body would simply present its views to parliament on matters relating to Aboriginal and Torres Strait Islander peoples, and may perform additional functions as parliament provides.

To be clear: a Voice to parliament is not simply about 'being heard'. It is about addressing the structural impediments that have rendered First Nations powerless. It is about empowerment, enabling First Nations to take a rightful place in the country.

'The Uluru Statement focuses on what we actually want. We want to have a say, we want to have a voice,' says Mick Gooda, former Aboriginal and Torres Strait Islander Social Justice Commissioner, who is part of the senior advisory group tasked with guiding the process towards developing options for a First Nations Voice to parliament.

In 2019, Minister for Indigenous Australians Ken Wyatt said that he hoped a referendum would be held within three years. At the same time, Scott Morrison rejected the Voice to parliament proposal, claiming it would constitute a third chamber.

In May 2020, Wyatt conceded that the referendum would be unlikely in this term of government—not only due to the pandemic, but because it was 'too important to fail'. 'I have always said that a referendum would be held when there was broad consensus on the wording, and when it had the best possible chance of success,' he told the *Guardian*.

Although the Prime Minister has since approved a new process led by Wyatt to develop a recognition proposal, there is still significant opposition, particularly from the right.

Mayor knows the referendum will be a hard win. Of the forty-four referendums held in Australia since 1901, just eight have been successful. 'If the referendum succeeds,' he tells me, 'and we have the courage to pursue it, it will speak with a mandate of the Australian people that must be listened to.'

We can look to the success of the Aboriginal community-controlled health sector's response to the pandemic to see how truly transformative a Voice to parliament could be.

'After centuries of what my people have endured since invasion, through the killing times and racial segregation, they are still generous enough and hopeful enough to imagine Australia can do better and be a better place,' Megan Davis writes in her essay 'The Long Road to Uluru'.

Australia can be a better place. The COVID-19 pandemic has shone light on the deep inequities that exist in Australia, the land of the 'fair go'. This is a time of awakening. It is a time of reckoning.

AN AUSTRALIAN RECKONING

'I can't breathe.'

Those were the last words of Black musician and father George Floyd before he was killed by a police officer in Minneapolis in May 2020. The officer knelt on Floyd's neck for nearly nine minutes. After months of the COVID-19 pandemic dominating global news and personal conversations, this tragic event shook the world to its core.

Australians were outraged. But Indigenous people also wondered where the outrage had been for the hundreds of Aboriginal and Torres Strait Islanders who'd lost their lives while in custody.

David Dungay Jr is just one of 434 (at the time of writing) Aboriginals who have died in custody. The Dunghutti man from Kempsey was an uncle and a poet. He died in Sydney's Long Bay jail in December 2015 after he was held down by six guards who rushed to his cell to stop him eating biscuits. The guards dragged him to another cell, held him down and had him injected twice with sedatives.

'I can't breathe.'

Those were his last words. An officer replied, 'If you can talk, you can breathe.'

Following the death of Floyd, tens of thousands of Australians across the country took to the streets to proclaim that 'Black Lives Matter', that 'tolerating racism is racism', and that 'injustice anywhere is a threat to justice everywhere'. It was an extraordinary act of solidarity in the midst of a pandemic.

Many said it was time for Australia's reckoning, that it was time for the country to hold a mirror up to itself. Who were we to condemn police brutality in another country when it was happening in our own backyard? Where had the rage, anger, frustration and empathy been for our own who had been murdered at the hands of those 'in charge'? Where was the anger at the systemic racism and disadvantage of our own country, the lucky country?

But a few protests are not, and will not be, enough to right the wrongs that continue to be inflicted.

Journalist Amy McQuire poses a pertinent question: if you do not support black rights here, in this country, how can you support them internationally?

'They [non-Indigenous Australians] are not "outraged" because they are not "shocked". There is nothing shocking about racist violence perpetrated by police, because it is normalised,' she writes in the *Canberra Times*. 'It is seen as legitimate violence. It is this legitimate violence that was not only used to steal the country and assert white dominance, but also maintain it through the oppression of Aboriginal people.'

It is to acknowledge and correct these wrongs that the Uluru Statement seeks to establish a Makarrata Commission to oversee agreement-making between First Nations and governments.

Makarrata—which is often used instead of 'treaty'—is a Yolngu word which, as Noel Pearson explains, 'captures the idea of two parties coming together after a struggle, healing the divisions of the past. It is about acknowledging something has been done wrong, and it seeks to make things right.'

The Makarrata Commission would have two goals. One is for First Nations to negotiate agreements with governments whereby 'both parties meet and share stories of the past and decide on how they will work together in the future in a stronger partnership'. The second is truth-telling about history, whereby the commission would provide 'an avenue for experiences to be articulated and heard, to create a path for reconciliation' between the First Nations and non-Indigenous Australians. Victoria is in the process of establishing Australia's first formal truth-telling process. More than thirty countries around the world have established such truth commissions, including Canada, New Zealand and South Africa.

Truth-telling is intrinsically linked to both the pandemic and the Black Lives Matter movement. The BLM movement tells the truth about Aboriginal and Torres Strait Islander experiences; the pandemic, on the other hand, has revealed the truth about *why* our Aboriginal communities are so vulnerable to the virus.

'A truth and reconciliation process is critical to Australia. Truth-telling is absolutely critical to healing our nation and raising awareness which so many people do not have,' says Noongar woman Dr Hannah McGlade, who is a senior Indigenous research fellow at Curtin University and a member of the UN Permanent Forum for Indigenous Peoples.

Storytelling is a central part of Indigenous culture—it not only influences the way people see the world and their place in it, but it fosters healing from past trauma. For non-Indigenous Australians, it provides a critical avenue to learn about the truths of this country. As writer Madeleine Wedesweiler puts it, 'Truth-telling [is the] key to liberating Australia from a deliberate silence.'

The way intergenerational trauma—from the ongoing effects of colonisation, loss of land, loss of language, erosion of culture, forced child removal, racism and discrimination—acts as a social determinant of health, employment, incarceration and living conditions has long been documented. The pervasive impact of intergenerational trauma—its origin and history neither understood nor respected by the non-Indigenous population—continues to reinforce the negative and harmful image of Aboriginal and Torres Strait Islander people in the media.

This has had devastating consequences. Just as 5D data has informed how Indigenous people view themselves, media coverage has reinforced the idea that Indigenous people are simply problems to be dealt with—by white people.

Enabling intergenerational survivors to participate in truth-telling could not only be healing, but would provide a powerful—and necessary—rebuttal to non-Indigenous Australians who think we should forget the devastating impacts of colonisation.

There is no doubt that constitutional recognition and a Voice to parliament—along with a Makarrata Commission—would be deeply transformative, and symbolically important to First Nations. But this is not the only work that needs to be done.

DOING THE WORK

To meet the targets of the Close the Gap agreement, we need huge legislative and policy reform, along with a pledge to shift the dynamic of power and an investment of resources.

While we wait for governments to act, we can look to Indigenous communities who are stepping up and stepping in to create a brighter future for their kids who are camping by the Darling river, and far beyond.

Change starts with education. As Malcolm X said in 1964, 'Education is the passport to the future, for tomorrow belongs to those who prepare for it today.'

'We want to see kids safe; we want to see kids educated,' says Mick Gooda, who was also the Co-Commissioner on the Royal Commission into the Protection and Detention of Children in the Northern Territory in 2016. 'We are not going to walk away from that, it's something everyone in our society is entitled to. But what does it mean for you? That's the next the question.'

For Gooda, this means providing Aboriginal kids with holistic education that understands and respects their background, nurtures their culture and provides support that goes well beyond what you would expect from a 'regular' school. It is also about family, community and accountability—showing up and doing the work.

According to the 2020 Close the Gap report, the attendance rate for Indigenous primary school students in 2019 was 85 per cent. By Year 10, that figure had dropped to 72 per cent—a gap of around 17 percentage points compared to non-Indigenous kids. Today, about 66 per cent of Indigenous students are completing twelve years of schooling, compared with 47 per cent in 2008.

But while the data is encouraging—more Indigenous kids are finishing school—it doesn't say anything about the quality of education, the school environment or their engagement. We are still losing way too many kids because the system isn't designed to support them.

Gooda cites the Murri School in Brisbane, an Indigenous-owned and -controlled independent school that was established in

1986. Ninety-five per cent of the school's students are Indigenous. It provides holistic education, which includes a focus on their health and providing family support. The school has psychologists, psychiatrists and speech pathologists, and culture is embedded in almost everything they do. The school is focused on holding kids and families to account but without being scathing and detrimental to a child's education. Gooda explains how it works in practice:

> At a mainstream school, if a kid turns up hungry or dirty, under the mandatory reporting rules, the principal will generally report directly to Child [Protective Services] and then they're in the system. Here, instead we go and speak to the parents, to the carer, and ask: what do you need here?
>
> For instance, just a couple of weeks ago, this family looked like they were about to be thrown out of their house. They had a house inspection coming up, so we went and got the lawns mowed and a skipper to take away the rubbish. Now, that's not something a regular school would do, but there are three kids involved. So, if they'd gotten thrown out of the house, we'd probably lose those kids. You do what you need to do to. We try to create a safe place for kids and families.

Emeritus professor at the University of Newcastle John Lester had a long career in Indigenous education, including as the first Indigenous TAFE principal in the country. As he tells me, 'I was the first Aboriginal no matter where I went.'

He tells me the problem with education is not school attendance, the focus of Close the Gap reports. Instead, it's about engagement.

'We are failing to engage Aboriginal children,' he says. 'The big push is getting bums on seats, but there's no point putting Aboriginal people in classrooms if they're not going to be engaged. What Aboriginal kids need are good quality teachers. If you're going to be a quality teacher, you need to have cultural acknowledgment; you need to understand the kids' culture you are teaching. If there are good quality teachers that will include Aboriginal people in the culture and therefore engage them, then they can keep going and they will succeed.'

Professor Lester, who was the first director of Aboriginal education in NSW back in 2005, wants quality teaching to be focused on urban areas where the majority of Aboriginal and Torres Strait Islanders live. That is not, however, to neglect remote areas—it is simply about generating change for the largest number of kids.

'Aboriginal kids are invisible in classrooms,' he says. 'They go there with the best advice from their parents, who tell them, "Don't draw attention to yourself, make sure you are good," and these kids go through school not making a fuss. So, the majority of them just sit in classrooms and fall through the system. I used to call those kids the Peter Brady kids; the invisible kids.

'What we've got to do if we want to turn this around is that we've got to address the eighty per cent of Aboriginal kids who live in major regional and urban areas, that's where we've got to make change happen and quality teaching needs to be at every one of those locations.'

He envisions going beyond the Murri School's model to establish specialist Aboriginal studies high schools. They would be similar to the specialist schools we have for agriculture, dance, music, sport. The schools would be for students who want to excel in Aboriginal studies. They wouldn't just be for Indigenous kids; they would be for anyone who has a keen interest in Aboriginal studies.

Professor Lester wants to sprinkle such schools around the country in urban and regional areas with large Aboriginal populations like the NSW Central Coast. 'These schools would not be exclusively Aboriginal, but the kids would need to understand that they're going to get the best quality Aboriginal education,' he says. 'They're going to be exposed to Aboriginal studies in the best way possible and we will be engaging kids because the kids will be getting high-quality education.'

Schools would also not just be staffed by Aboriginal teachers. They would be staffed by the highest-quality Aboriginal studies teachers—teachers who can engage students and who understand history and culture.

With the pandemic forcing schoolkids and university students to learn from home, a revolution in online learning was also sparked. In such an environment, these specialist schools could also use their expertise to teach kids from other schools, too. So, rather than local schools teaching Aboriginal studies, kids could tap in via the web to learn from specialist schools.

It could be transformative, for both Indigenous and non-Indigenous students and their families.

'Kids are taught about the oldest continuous living culture in the world through colouring in boomerangs, didgeridoos and kangaroos year after year,' Professor Lester says. 'Let's use this virus and the stimulus around it to build these special schools, these hub schools, which can go on to serve as Aboriginal studies nests.'

Professor Lester's idea is just one of many to transform the education system in Australia. If we can have specialist schools for agriculture, dance, music, sport, why not for Aboriginal studies?

Historically, schooling for our Aboriginal kids has been used as a tool of control by non-Indigenous Australians, rather than as a tool of freedom, of emancipation, of opportunity, like it is for the rest of us Australians. Throughout the education system, Aboriginal and Torres Strait Islander people must be empowered to practice self-determination.

If our vision is to build an Australia that is just and equitable and—importantly—reconciled, then creating an education system that is built to respect, nurture, embody and celebrate Indigenous culture is vital.

In her essay 'A Rightful Path', Sandra Phillips, associate professor and associate dean of Indigenous engagement at the University of Queensland, and Wakka Wakka and Gooreng Gooreng woman, writes, 'We continue to participate in mainstream education as descendants of the world's oldest living culture while carving out success on mainstream terms sometimes complementary with, and sometimes antithetical to, our cultural inheritance and our future interests. Getting that balancing act right takes all our guile.'

It is this exact sentiment that is echoed in the Uluru Statement from the Heart: 'When we have power over our destiny our children will flourish. They will walk in two worlds and their culture will be a gift to this country.'

•••

Prisons are coronavirus Petri dishes. Coronavirus has spread rapidly in countries where people are locked up, not locked down, where overcrowding is pervasive, where people are given very little in the way of protecting themselves against disease, and where people already live with multiple illnesses and are highly vulnerable to more.

Australia thought it had been spared the worst of the virus. That was until it came back with a vengeance in Victoria and we went into Stage 4 lockdown. News soon arrived of COVID-19 infiltrating several Victorian prisons. Fortunately, unlike other parts of the world, prisons didn't become deadly COVID-19 hotspots, despite calls to release prisoners falling on deaf ears.

Dr McGlade uses the term 'mass incarceration'—which is typically used in the US context to refer to the excessively high rate of Black Americans in prison—to describe the situation for Aboriginal and Torres Strait Islanders here.

'Mass incarceration is a way of speaking about the way our people are subjected to criminalisation,' she says. 'We have to use this term because this is not about the individual, this is not about an individualised problem of people who commit more crimes. This is about racism that is systemic and structural within the criminal justice system. It's not something Australia wants to pay attention to.'

On average across the country, Indigenous children are seventeen times more likely to be imprisoned than non-Indigenous kids. Dr McGlade tells me that in Western Australia, Aboriginal children are fifty times more likely than non-Indigenous youth to be incarcerated.

'It is just this constant surveillance of Aboriginal kids,' she says.

We are talking about a country that has imprisoned an Aboriginal child for accepting a stolen Freddo frog. We are talking about a country that has failed to act on advice to raise the age at which children can be imprisoned from ten to fourteen years. The failure to act is not only inherently racist, it constitutes a vicious attack on the health of some of our country's most disadvantaged kids. It sends a very clear message to our kids that we do not care.

It is a blight on this nation.

But again, while we wait for governments to act—to recognise the racism and discrimination engrained in our systems and institutions and dismantle them—Indigenous communities are stepping up and leading the way in finding solutions to prevent kids from ending up entwined in the criminal justice system.

In 2013, the far western NSW town of Bourke was labelled the 'most dangerous in the world' after it topped the state in six out of eight major crime categories. It received the title when its per capita crime rate was compared with United Nations data, thereby revealing it to allegedly be more dangerous than any other country on the planet.

The label was dangerously damaging to a town that already had a brutal reputation. Bourke is one of the most disadvantaged communities in Australia, with high rates of family violence and long-term unemployment, and the highest rate of juvenile convictions in the state. More than one in three in the town are Indigenous.

But by coming together, the community has turned things around. In 2015, after two years of community meetings and hours of strategising, Bourke became the first major town in Australia to implement community-led justice reinvestment. The Maranguka Justice Reinvestment project (Maranguka translates to 'caring for others' in the Ngemba language) is a local initiative that redirects the resources spent on policing and punishment to projects that actually work to prevent offending behaviour. It has empowered the community to develop local solutions to their issues.

The project is a model of Indigenous self-governance, which has enabled the community to coordinate the right mix and timing of services through an Aboriginal-owned and -led team that works in partnership with government and non-government agencies, according to Just Reinvest NSW, which runs the project.

One of the key initiatives of the project has been to help young people obtain driver licences, thereby reducing the number of kids arrested for driving without one. Off-duty police officers volunteered in the program and helped young learners to get their hours up. The impact has been profound. Between 2015 and 2017, there was a 72 per cent reduction in the number of people under twenty-five arrested for driving without a licence.

'Therein lies the power of community,' Gooda says, who has long championed community-led justice reinvestment as the key to addressing the unacceptably high rate of incarceration.

A recent impact assessment found that since the initiation of the project, there's been an 18 per cent reduction in major offences, a 39 per cent reduction in domestic violence assaults, a 42 per cent drop in days spent in custody, and a 31 per cent increase in Year 12 retention.

Whether we are responding to a pandemic or to bushfires, we know a united community—one that is empowered to put forward community-owned and -led solutions—can be, and will be, powerful.

•••

Throughout the pandemic, we have been constantly reminded that we are in it together. As a community, we of course like to believe that we are—and as the proliferation of mutual aid has shown, we are united. Together we stand.

But on a grander scale, we are not all in it together.

The phrase does not reflect lived experience. It ignores the deep-rooted, disproportionate realities of structural inequality and structural violence that impact our Indigenous population on a daily basis (and other marginalised groups, too).

The COVID-19 pandemic has not only exposed the yawning health disparities our Aboriginal and Torres Strait Islander population face, but it has also exposed Australia's appalling inability to address the social determinants of health and wellbeing. It has made evident the very reasons *why* our First Nations people are so vulnerable to this deadly virus. It has also revealed the shortcomings of the systems and institutions that are in place ostensibly to protect us.

But unlike past plagues, this time the Aboriginal community-controlled health sector and First Nations communities across the continent showed who is best placed to solve the issues that confront them. It is not non-Indigenous Australians.

Constitutional change through the realisation of the Uluru Statement from the Heart will create enduring structural change for First Nations people. It is not the only change that needs to happen, but it is perhaps the most critical.

'When our voice is protected in the constitution from the vagaries of ideology and party politics, we will be heard, and we can have a fair and truthful relationship with the people of Australia,' Professor Megan Davis writes in the *Monthly*. 'It is only then that the acknowledgment of country will become less ritualistic and performative. It will no longer be an Australian welcoming; it will be an Australian homecoming.'

If now is not the time for the Uluru Statement to be realised, for it to move us all closer to being it in together—for the present crisis and those that we cannot yet see or imagine—then when is?

4 | EDUCATION AND HEALTH

> 'One learns, I would hope, to discover what is right, what needs to be righted—through work, through action.'
>
> DANIEL BERRIGAN, 1971

In early March 2020, Vathna's father flew from the capital of Cambodia, Phnom Penh, which sits at the junction of the Mekong and Tonlé Sap rivers, to Melbourne. He was travelling to Australia to help his daughter settle into her first year at Monash University. As the duo traipsed around the city's centre, situated by the Yarra River, they were among the few people to wear masks. The racist comments they endured came at a time when the coronavirus was being described by some of the world's leaders as the 'Chinese virus'.

'I understood that this type of thing would happen in Australia,' eighteen-year-old Vathna tells me. 'This type of thing happens every day. Because of the whole racist thing, it actually got scary going outside alone. It's normal, which is stupid.'

There were no restrictions at the time, but Australia was only days away from entering lockdown. The closest Vathna would get to a real classroom at Monash would be to admire it from a distance. She had applied to study psychology. Like most teenagers, she didn't really know what path her career would or could take. The options were overwhelming. She was fascinated, though, by the human psyche and thought that whatever she learned could be applied to any turn her career—and life—would take.

Vathna was acutely aware of what families living in countries like Cambodia and Nepal had to give up in order to enable a child to attend university in a distant land, where a sip of coffee costs more than what many people earn in a day. She expressed gratitude to her parents and made a commitment to throw herself into her studies to do them—and herself—proud.

'For the majority of international students here, their families have given up as much as they can so they can get here. People sell their house to come to Australia. I think a lot of it is that parents believe so much in their children that they give as much as possible,' she says. 'I want to bring the knowledge I get from Australia back to my country. I don't want to leave my country behind.'

When first semester began, week one was online. Week two, students were told, would be on campus. Things were looking up. But as the second week began, face-to-face teaching was cancelled. It was back to virtual learning as university lecturers scrambled to make their classes as online-friendly and engaging as possible.

For Australian students, and the hundreds of thousands of international students who had uprooted their lives to study in a faraway country, this was not how they imagined university life would be. No socialising, no making new friends, no pub trivia nights, no face-to-face lectures or tutorials, no libraries, no sports, no clubs. For lecturers and tutors too, this wasn't how they envisioned teaching their classes.

New technologies held many promises, but the transition couldn't be done overnight. And with the over-casualisation of the university sector, already precarious jobs were looking even more insecure. By July 2020, Monash University had cut almost three hundred jobs.

'The quality of education is not what I expected it to be. The university has cut funding and now we just have one lecturer and one tutor for the whole course,' Vathna says. 'Most of it is just self-studying. It's not much fun. You get unmotivated doing online classes.'

Vathna's concerns about the declining quality of teaching is not just a result of the pandemic; university professors had already seen it happening for years.

'We have moved to a more bureaucratic model of teaching with less personal interaction, with more dumbed down, trivialised assignments,' says Salvatore Babones, globalisation expert and associate professor of sociology at the University of Sydney.

As Australia went into lockdown and hundreds of thousands of people became unemployed overnight, Prime Minister Scott Morrison told international students in April that if they were not in a position to support themselves, 'then there is the alternative for them to return to their home countries'. *We have taken your money, and now you are free to go home; you are on your own.*

International students, with no access to the federal government's welfare programs, including the new JobSeeker and JobKeeper initiatives, had to face the pandemic without the financial safety net available to other Australian citizens and residents. (Australians studying in many countries overseas were offered wage help.) There are more than half a million international students in Australia, and many were left without the security of a casual or part-time job when the virus struck. The impact was profound and visible. Lines of international university students snaked around Melbourne's city centre, queuing for free food given out by charities. 'These are international students who are having to go to food banks to stay alive,' says Katharine Betts, adjunct associate professor of sociology at Swinburne University. Stories of students living together in overcrowded accommodation, living out of their cars, becoming homeless, made the papers each week.

Were we really all in this together?

With but a few flights leaving every day, and with students already having built their lives here thanks to the sacrifices of their families, going home was an impossible decision. Vathna thought about it. She mapped out the few possible (and exorbitantly priced) flight routes home. Her parents begged her not to come back. *Stay in Australia, it is better for your future*, they told her. *It is safer there too*, they said. She wondered what would happen if she left. *Will I be able to continue my studies? Will I be able to return to the place that I now call home? What will happen to the huge amount of money my family has invested in my future? How can I ever justify leaving?*

'There's this feeling that because we're not Australian, then the government doesn't have to protect us,' Vathna says. 'Australians generally assume that we're very rich. I understand it's our choice that we came here, but without international students, Australia is losing a lot of money. Australia is very dependent on international students. It's not bad to have international students—I believe it enriches the learning environment—but the country should not be so dependent on us.'

PROFITS AND LOSSES

In recent decades there has been an immense global surge in the number both of universities and of students. It's an expansion that

British academic Stefan Collini, in his book *Speaking of Universities*, describes as 'an expansion that, in purely numerical terms, quite dwarfs anything that has happened in the previous eight centuries or so during which versions of this curious institution have existed'. But the changes have not merely been numerical—the whole ecology of higher education has been transformed. And nowhere is this more evident than in Australia. 'The pace and scale of change have produced a sense of disorientation, an uneasy feeling that, as a society, we may be losing our once-familiar understanding of the nature and role of universities, yet we have not replaced it with anything better,' Collini writes.

Historically, universities have been melting pots of culture and ideas; they were respected institutions where the elite would gather to create, discuss, debate and disperse knowledge. 'Society,' Collini writes, 'was respectful of universities as one of the chief homes of a traditionally conceived "culture", which it was the aspiration of the historically less privileged classes to acquire.' Is today's society as respectful of universities as it once was?

'Universities everywhere have the primary mission of educating mostly young people, though, increasingly, working professionals as well, in their own country,' Babones says. 'The University of Sydney, for example, was started as a place for the youth—for young men, let's face it—at the time in Sydney, to have further education without having to go overseas.

'But,' he says, 'in Australia we have seen such a push towards the generation of revenue from international students that it has affected the core mission of our universities—which has been transformed from educating local students to generating revenue to support research.'

•••

In the early 1970s, the government of the time—the Whitlam Labor government—abolished university fees after a push to make tertiary education more accessible. The decision significantly increased university participation, but free education didn't last long. By the mid-1980s, the transition from an elite tertiary education system to a mass higher education system was no longer considered sustainable. Instead, a subsequent Labor government reintroduced fees for university education and set up the loan system that is still in place: the Higher Education Contribution Scheme (now called HECS-HELP), which enables students to study at public universities (and some private ones too) and defer their loan repayments until they begin professional employment and earn over a certain threshold (today, that's $46,620 per annum).

It was at this time that Australian National University economist Helen Hughes—among others—argued that higher education could be 'turned from a liability into an asset by charging fees to international students', writes Hannah Forsyth in her essay 'Disinterested Scholars or Interested Parties? The Public's Investment in Self-interested Universities'. The opportunity to charge international students large fees to study in the lucky country was too enticing to ignore.

These transformations happened under the watch of Labor education minister John Dawkins, who also decided to merge all Colleges of Advanced Education—teaching institutions that did not conduct research—into a uniform higher education system. This resulted in the creation of sixteen new universities, and the introduction of a series of protocols universities had to use to justify courses and research. The impact of his sweeping changes cannot be overstated.

The editors of *The Dawkins Revolution: 25 Years On* write that

Dawkins 'turned colleges into universities, free education into HECS, elite education into mass education, local focuses into international outlooks, vice-chancellors into corporate leaders, teachers into teachers and researchers...He remodelled higher education and how it was funded in only a few years.' Higher education was now considered a privilege, not a freely accessible public good.

A public good has two characteristics: it is non-rivalrous (when it is consumed, it doesn't reduce the amount available to others) and it is non-excludable (individuals cannot be effectively excluded from its use). Public goods enrich society and they are an absolute necessity; they are tied largely to civic standing, responsibilities and duties—a particular type of social contract. Education must be a public good, not a commodity nor a private benefit. But how do you define public goods when domestic and overseas actors are entwined? What is the nature of the social contract in that sense?

As Margaret Thornton, editor of *Through a Glass Darkly: The Social Sciences Look at the Neoliberal University*, writes, 'Public universities were not instantaneously privatised as a result of the neoliberal turn...Instead, the process has been an incremental one, involving the increasing application of business practices to them as if they were for-profit corporations. In other words, they have been "corporatised".'

The university under this model has not only been corporatised, it has been marketised, commercialised, casualised and manageralised. It has been bastardised.

Australia has the lion's share of full-fee international students in higher education across the OCED countries. Its vice-chancellors are on salaries comparable to top ASX chief executive officers; education has become Australia's third-biggest export 'industry', worth $23 billion. More than one in four university students are from overseas.

At some universities, including RMIT, Monash and the University of Wollongong, more than 40 per cent of students are international. More than 40 per cent of all international students in Australia are from China. Ten years ago, Australia had three universities in the global top hundred, according to the Academic Ranking of World Universities; today, there are seven. All seven are part of the eight research-intensive universities that make up the Group of Eight. The only countries that have more universities in the top hundred than Australia are the United States and the United Kingdom—countries not only with populations far greater than our small island nation, but with far more universities. It's a phenomenon Babones describes as a 'sign of pathology' because 'it means that resources are being dramatically misallocated'.

'Starting around the year two thousand, there was an implicit decision to allow Australia to take on more international students,' says the vice-chancellor of the Australian National University, Brian Schmidt. 'We became very competitive in the international world and we got into a mode where we took more and more students and the universities received pretty much flat funding for domestic activities, and I would even argue decreased funding within the research portfolio.'

(In 1990, 86 per cent of the universities' funding came from the Commonwealth and 14 per cent from other sources. Now some 30 per cent of funding comes from the federal government.)

'And since brand is determined a lot by research, you get this weird feedback where international students are paying for research in a way that does not happen in the rest of the world. As a nation, the government has systematically retreated from funding research and has allowed that to be funded by international student fees. There are a lot of people saying "how dare you be so reliant on China and international student fees" but, well, I'm afraid it's been an un-publicly declared agreement between the government and the university sector to do it this way. We both knew what was going on, we didn't talk about, we just let it happen.'

Universities have often hired vice-chancellors with substantial managerial expertise but without sufficient academic credentials to be appointed professors, with the sole mission of improving rankings. That is how universities attract international students.

In his book *The Tyranny of Metrics*, historian Jerry Muller writes:

> The most characteristic feature of metric fixation is the aspiration to replace judgement based on experience with standardized measurement. For judgment is understood to be personal, subjective, and self-interested. Metrics, by contrast, are supposed to provide information that is hard and objective. The strategy is to improve institutional efficiency by offering rewards to those whose metrics are highest, or whose benchmarks or targets have been reached, and to penalise those who fall behind.

How do you measure a university's 'success'? Teaching is difficult to measure so performance on rankings has become the gold standard. How do you rise up in the rankings? Research output. Research is what counts for the Group of Eight research-intensive universities—and those other universities longing to join their ranks. Australian universities have aggressively made their way up international rankings by producing high-quality research—but that research requires money. A lot of it. Yet according to the Academic Ranking of World Universities—the most prestigious ranking system—not all research is worth measuring. It ranks universities primarily based on publications in the Web of Science database, which includes the sciences but not the humanities. It might be worth pondering why Scott Morrison's government decided to drastically increase the cost of a humanities degree by 113 per cent, from $20,400 to $43,500.

'So, you want to succeed in those rankings, what do you do? You hire a lot of scientists,' Babones says. 'You hire globally prominent researchers on research-only contracts funded by student tuition fees and international students' fees. You pump out lots of journal articles. And that helps you rise in the rankings.

'In Australia, these positions have been funded out of current revenues and that's why there's a crisis right now: because universities have made massive financial commitments to researchers who don't teach. Now the money that generates the revenue to make that possible has suddenly disappeared and they're loath to give up researchers because the researchers are the basis of their ranking success.'

A crisis indeed. And one that is estimated to cost $16 billion in losses by 2023.

What has been the impact of this pursuit of 'excellence'? Who has suffered? What has suffered? The paradox is that while we still need and want research in the humanities and social sciences (despite some conservatives saying otherwise), overall funding has been reduced in favour of areas perceived to have greater value in the market: computer science, engineering, microbiology. This is to the detriment not only of the academics who have dedicated their careers to advancing research in their specific fields, but of Australia's knowledge base as whole. But the humanities not only provide tremendous cultural and social value—they also produce tangible economic outcomes. For example, in 2018, the creative arts sector directly contributed $14.7 billion to the economy. The sector employs almost 200,000 people—far more than coal.

'The kind of research that might be useful for policymakers in Australia—people are being encouraged not to do it and instead to do the stuff that will get into high-ranking international journals because that's hard currency,' Betts says. 'I think this is the way in which the system has kind of lost its focus on what it's there for: to educate domestic students so they can have a satisfying life because their horizons have been broadened.'

Today, universities are full of non-teaching academics whose primary purpose is to research. Teaching academics, on the other hand, continue to put one foot in the front of the other, determined to keep going despite the increasing casualisation of their sector, which has been reduced to contract work and perpetual financial insecurity.

'The whole rationale for the research university is that good researchers make better teachers because they bring the most advanced concepts into the classroom,' Babones says. 'Once those functions are separated, I don't think there's any rationale for the University of Sydney, or any other university, having research institutes with dozens of people who don't teach. Why should universities be engaged in research-only activities? This is the fundamental question.'

Who is research for? Who does it benefit? Who *should* it benefit? What institutions should be pursuing Australia's research interests and who should be funding it? Is it moral, is it ethical, that the onus has been placed on international students? We do not need to look far to see how the federal government's position on research and science has contributed to the crisis our universities find themselves in. This is a government that since 2013, when the Coalition came to power, has continued to make cuts to research and development. In 2015, for example, the federal government spent just 0.4 per cent of GDP on research and development, putting Australia at the bottom of the list, next to Greece, which has been crippled by a deep and long-term financial crisis.

In her Quarterly Essay *The Coal Curse*, Judith Brett outlines how, under Tony Abbott's prime ministership, denial and scepticism about climate change spread to science more generally. We can look to Abbott's criticisms of ANU for divesting from fossil-fuel industries and the Liberals' secret rejections of eleven grants over multiple years recommended by the Australian Research Council for research in history, music and art history as evidence of the flourishing culture wars. We can also look to the decision to exclude universities from JobKeeper and the latest education reforms—the so-called 'job-ready graduates' package—which will significantly hike up the cost of a humanities degree, withdraw financial support from students who fail half of their first-year courses and ultimately reduce the government's contribution towards Commonwealth Supported Places for further evidence.

'The Australian politicians' ritual denunciation of selected research topics receiving grants would be amusing were it not symbolic of a deeper danger. A pluralist democracy is underpinned by freedom of inquiry,' Glenn Withers writes in his essay 'The State of the Universities'. These moves—and many more—send a strong message: we will not support institutions that do not propagate a conservative ideology.

•••

What will the pandemic mean for Australia's universities? It appears that none of the country's forty universities will be left unscathed.

The pandemic has not only tested the resilience of some of our oldest and most important institutions, it has forced them to confront long-standing challenges far beyond the scope of the international-student conundrum, from the over-casualisation of the workforce, to elitism and exclusion, and proposed tuition-fee hikes. These issues are past boiling point—they are now impossible to ignore.

The most immediate impact of the pandemic will be the loss of international student fee revenue, which at some universities accounted for nearly 40 per cent of total income. Without access to JobKeeper (the government made three changes to the wage subsidy to ensure universities were not eligible), universities have had to make massive job cuts (up to 21,000) and several regional universities are planning to shut campuses. There is much at stake for Australia's largest service-based export, which, in 2019, directly and indirectly contributed $37.6 billion to the economy.

At the time of writing, though the border remains shut, there are plans to slowly allow international students into the country. Whether they will choose—or can afford—to come back is another question. Many suggest Australia cannot expect Chinese students to continue to flock to its universities. With the expected loss of international student revenue—whose fees enabled universities to fund research and build fancy buildings—who will step in to fill the void? Is there the chance of universities becoming fully corporatised? Will the next generation of students attend Google's University of Melbourne or Amazon's University of Sydney?

Adam Bandt, leader of the Greens and federal MP for Melbourne, fears that the pandemic has given the federal government the impetus to begin charging domestic students upfront fees. 'I fear they [the government] are trying to starve universities to the point where they demand the right to charge upfront fees—not just for international students, but for local students as well,' he says. 'I think the argument from the government about universities' reliance on overseas students is a very sinister and disingenuous one because it overlooks the fact that the Liberals pushed them to that point.'

Higher education has already been transformed from a predominantly public good to a privatised one, which not only has severe ramifications for the future, but also for the workings of democracy. As we witness the erosion of democratic norms and the rise of authoritarianism across the world, universities have never been so important. Universities are critical in the fight to support and preserve democracy.

What would it be like if we began treating universities as public goods? As institutions characterised by the pursuit of higher learning and research for the public's benefit? It would mean that universities would not be reliant on cash cows, but rather properly and adequately funded. They would be autonomous, creative learning environments that were free to conduct independent research. They would be accountable to the public and not motivated by profits. All these elements are central to shoring up the public benefit of universities to society.

'We should have free education,' Bandt says. 'We have to treat universities as public goods, and then, when they are fully funded and are not reliant on fees from international students, then we can have a discussion about what is the appropriate number of places to offer overseas students and the conditions on which they should be offered.'

Should we not want to live in a society where everyone is entitled to a world-class higher education? We have universal primary and secondary education so why not higher education? In a country that prides itself on the creation and dispersal of knowledge as a way to increase 'productivity', why do we exclude those who want to pursue a degree because they cannot afford it, because they cannot access it? We can afford to provide free higher education—if we choose. We can map out a future where international students do not fund our research output and the fancy university buildings that adorn glossy pamphlets.

Universities perform about 90 per cent of the research undertaken in Australia and 43 per cent of all our nation's applied research. How will universities continue to afford to pursue high-quality research—the very thing that has propelled seven of the Group of Eight universities into the top hundred?

Research of all kinds must be respected, and it must be supported. We are at a critical moment, when our universities can reshape themselves to become more relevant on local and national levels, to contribute solutions to pressing problems. In the face of our climate-change emergency, this is even more urgent. But it will require new ideas. New ways of recognising and supporting higher education are critical for discovery and innovation, fostering cross-cultural learning and building community resilience.

It will require understanding that our current model is simply not fit for a post-pandemic world, nor is it equipped for other crises we cannot yet see or imagine.

'Universities are places where research and teaching coexist, and are meant to coexist, to look at long-term problems, to make sure that the bleeding edge of knowledge is transferred to the next generation, and that knowledge is generated,' ANU Vice-Chancellor Brian Schmidt says. 'We need a certain amount of absolutely world-leading basic academic research in a whole wealth of disciplines, from the humanities through to the fundamental sciences. The government should figure out what percentage of GDP it wants to spend…and [it] should provide universities autonomy.'

While modes and norms of teaching and learning are changing, the nature of work is also changing. Universities and other higher education institutions will have to evolve and adapt to this new reality. We were woefully unprepared for a pandemic. We must be prepared for the future. It is coming. Quickly.

ON THE FRONTLINE

The first case of COVID-19 was confirmed in Australia in late January 2020, in a man who flew from Wuhan to Melbourne. Just over a month later, the first case of community transmission was confirmed.

Australia has a world-class health-care system, but it had not run a large-scale national pandemic exercise since 2008, when the global financial crisis hit and Australian politics descended into chaos. But then in 2009, as if to remind the world that nature is more powerful than politics, the H1N1 virus, which caused the swine flu pandemic, spread rapidly across the world. It wasn't, however, as deadly as expected, and subsequently gave credence to the growing belief among the political elites that pandemics were not as dangerous as infectious disease experts predicted them to be. How very wrong they were.

The failure to continue pandemic practice exercises, some suggest, contributed to confusion in the early days of Australia's coronavirus response. This confusion proved deadly when 2700 passengers on the *Ruby Princess* cruise ship were allowed to disembark in Sydney in March 2020 without proper screening. Many coughing, sneezing and spluttering people left the cruise ship bound for buses, trains, and domestic and international travel. At least nine hundred people later tested positive. Twenty-eight died. These were lives that were cut tragically short, leaving families without mothers, daughters, fathers, sons, brothers, sisters. An inquiry into the disaster heard of the confusion and conflicting information from different authorities. It found that NSW Health's decision to classify the ship as 'low risk' was as 'inexplicable as it is unjustifiable'. Even when institutions claimed they were pandemic 'ready'—like the Sydney aged-care facility Newmarch House did in a self-assessment eighteen days before seventeen residents succumbed to the virus—confusion prevailed. It was later revealed that the self-assessment guidelines it used caused the facility to treat COVID-19 'as a flu-like illness'.

Newmarch House was, of course, not fully ready for the pandemic (indeed, the system which it operates even serves to undermine pandemic preparedness and readiness) but an independent review found that confusion about which state or federal government health authority held executive authority worsened the deadly outbreak.

The pandemic has taught us many things, one of which is that pandemic preparedness and response are global public goods. Particularly in the face of climate change, we must be asking critical questions about our future. Are we prepared for the next pandemic? How can we prepare for diseases that we cannot yet see or imagine? How can we, how do we, protect our population? What steps can we take today to create a safer future for us all?

•••

Our pandemic preparedness shortfalls aside, Australia privileged science over politics to place medical experts at the centre of our response to the virus. We listened to the experts, and we chose evidence-based policy over opinion-based policy. The federal government worked hand-in-hand with the states and territories to beef up laboratory testing capacity, prepare public hospitals (private ones too), train healthcare staff, set up isolation facilities, deploy robust test, trace and isolate systems, roll out public-health campaigns, and lock down the country. As we watched news of rising cases in the United States, the United Kingdom, Italy, Brazil and India, we thought, *Aren't we lucky that we live in Australia.* At the time of writing, fewer than a thousand people have died in Australia, while more than fifty-two thousand have died in the United Kingdom. But the real question is: how many of the deaths here could have been prevented? And why are we choosing to compare ourselves to Europe instead of Taiwan, Thailand, New Zealand and Hong Kong, countries that have all performed better than we have? Did we do all that we were capable of doing?

First Nations communities across Australia warned of impending disaster, of communities literally being decimated by the virus simply because physical distancing and hand-washing—two of the best defences against the disease—were impossible in some places. But the pandemic didn't just expose the deep-rooted health inequalities that exist between Indigenous and non-Indigenous Australians: it exposed the inequalities that exist across the entire social hierarchy, and laid bare the conditions that imperil specific communities. Despite what we are told, we are *not* in this together. The pandemic has not been the great equaliser. Rather, it has been the great revealer, casting light on the ugly and uneven facade of structural inequality.

How can people living in overcrowded homes physically distance and isolate themselves when their living and working arrangements make that impossible? How can people living rough protect themselves? And what about those in prisons who already live in conditions ripe for the spread of disease? How do people frequently wash their hands when they do not have the privilege of running water, nor access to hand sanitiser? How can we expect people to be concerned about a virus when they are anxious about where their next pay cheque will come from? These are confronting questions, even more so for a country like Australia, a wealthy nation that prides itself on being the 'lucky country'. We seem blind to the irony in the title of Donald Horne's celebrated book, which was a plea for Australia to wake up to its mediocrity.

As we patted our backs for a job well done, and life began to regain some semblance of normalcy, major gaps in our hotel quarantine program (outsourced to poorly trained, poorly paid private security providers) emerged. These breaches ultimately led to Melbourne—and then, a few weeks later, Victoria—being locked down again. An inquiry into the catastrophic failure of the program found that more than 90 per cent of cases across the state during its second wave could, as of August 2020, be linked to an outbreak at just one hotel. It was no surprise when Melbourne's infection rate began skyrocketing.

In July, COVID-19 was confirmed in residents living in public housing in North Melbourne. One brisk Saturday afternoon, three thousand people living across nine public housing towers were, without forewarning, placed under house arrest to help stem the spread of the virus. Hundreds of police were dispatched to stand guard. This was not a lockdown; it was a lock-in. The residents were held captive. Would a police-enforced lockdown without warning have happened in one of Melbourne's more affluent suburbs? For the residents—who come from diverse backgrounds and ethnicities, including refugees and asylum seekers who have fled unspeakable violence and war, Indigenous people, and people experiencing severe mental illness and family violence—the heavy-handed response was deeply traumatic. It also illustrated how the conditions in which people are born, grow, live, work and age fuel the spread of disease.

In these communities, up to ten people share a single small flat. Physical distancing is impossible. Rates of unemployment are high and income is low, English is perhaps people's third or fourth language, access to education is limited and internet access is poor (many residents found out about the lock-in on television and didn't understand what was happening). In total, more than 350 people were infected. When the government delivered inappropriate supplies (including non-halal food) to those trapped inside their homes, the community on the outside banded together. People from all walks of life donated food and other essential supplies. Their support was so generous that organisations had to start turning people away.

The situation raised critical questions about the state of public housing, not just as a health risk, but as a propagator of social inequality and division. More broadly, the pandemic raised concerns about the scale of homelessness and rough sleeping across the country. Dr Ilan Wiesel from the school of geography at the University of Melbourne says a culture of paternalism towards public-housing tenants has run deep in institutions for decades. The system that justifies short-term tenancies by presenting tenants as a 'burden on public resources', Dr Wiesel writes, ignores the very fact that tenants are locked out of 'labour markets by structural forces rather than by individual choice'. 'These practices reflect a prevailing neoliberal ideology that suggests full citizenship rights are reserved to those who are economically productive, earn wage income and own property,' he writes for the University of Melbourne's *Pursuit*, a source of commentary on COVID-19. 'Public housing tenants, in contrast, are expected to simply be grateful to the state for providing them shelter, however inadequate, and in accepting such "charity" they give up on basic rights and freedoms that other citizens enjoy. The remedy for such paternalism isn't the dismantling of public housing.'

Dr Wiesel calls for a deep transformation of public housing and community-housing governance so that tenants have a meaningful voice in decisions concerning their homes and their lives. Underlying these practical steps—which include investing in tenant advocacy groups, choice-based lettings and the appointment of tenant representatives—is the fundamental belief that housing is a human right and that having a say in the decisions affecting one's life is critical for democracy to function. Not only do we desperately need to transform the public housing sector that we already have, but we urgently need to build more social housing for families and individuals to reduce homelessness and rough sleeping. More than 140,000 people are on social housing waitlists and 120,000 people are without a home every night, with warnings that the situation will continue to worsen. But in a sign that leaders are waking up to the problem, in November 2020 the Victorian government committed $5.3 billion towards building twelve thousand social-housing homes throughout Melbourne and regional areas. Two thousand of the new homes will be for people living with mental illness and a thousand will be for Indigenous Victorians.

AGED CARE: A BROKEN SYSTEM

It is often said that the said true measure of any society is how well it treats its most vulnerable members. In 2018, after horrific evidence of abuse and neglect in residential aged care came to light, Scott Morrison announced the Royal Commission into Aged Care Quality and Safety. The commission, which is still ongoing, examined 'images of people with maggots feeding in open sores' and found that 'dreadful food, nutrition and hydration, and insufficient attention to oral health' had led to 'widespread malnutrition, excruciating dental and other pain, and secondary conditions'.

What we have done to some of our most vulnerable community members is immoral, unethical and simply unforgivable. How 'well' we treat our elderly is an indictment of our nation. But the revelations do not seem to have been appalling or disgusting enough to garner change. So when COVID-19 hit, it wasn't long before more horrific stories and images emerged from residential aged care. The *Guardian* revealed that a ninety-five-year-old woman in a Melbourne aged-care home ravaged by coronavirus was left to languish with ants crawling from a wound on her leg. Other residents hadn't had food or water for eighteen hours. There were faeces on the floor. This time, though, there was nowhere to hide. The elderly were dying in droves and the nation was watching the tragedy unfold.

'Homer Simpson could have seen the catastrophe in aged care coming with COVID-19 because it was there in your face,' says Professor Joseph Ibrahim, head of the health law and ageing unit at Monash University and an expert witness at the aged-care royal commission. 'All I know is that you can't accept things as they are, because they're not right.'

In 1997, Australia's aged-care system was transformed into a free-market model that, in Professor Ibrahim's words, was 'ill-conceived and never worked'. In 2011, the full funding and policy responsibility for aged care moved from state and territory level to the federal government. Today, the sector represents a multi-billion-dollar industry that is predominantly publicly funded. But despite the government being the primary funder and regulator of aged care, the combination of high levels of mismanagement and big profits for the owners of residential homes has meant that even throwing money at the problem hasn't been enough to prevent COVID-19 from sweeping through, taking victims at every turn.

At the time of writing, the death toll in residential aged care, driven by the situation in Victoria, has skyrocketed beyond 680. Hundreds more are infected, including more than a thousand health-care workers. In Victoria, the government says up to 80 per cent of health-care workers have contracted the virus. That three-quarters of the country's deaths have occurred in such facilities gives Australia one of the highest rates worldwide of deaths in residential aged care as a percentage of total deaths. What has been the cause?

'I don't think anything has gone wrong per se, it was already wrong,' Professor Ibrahim says. 'There were not enough workers to start with; the workforce that exists doesn't have the training for a contemporary aged-care system. They're not equipped to manage disease complexity and they're not equipped to deal with ethical human rights issues. So then COVID-19 arrives and there are not enough staff, staff who don't know what they're doing, staff who haven't been trained in infection control. Audits have been demonstrating gaps in infection control for years—gaps in the delivery of clinical care for years—with the government assigning responsibility directly to the provider with no form or plan and the stipulation that they need to get their own people, their own swabs, and to negotiate with the acute hospital in the case of an outbreak and manage it themselves.

'Residential care is free-market-driven and sold as accommodation, when, in fact, it's far closer to health care now than it's ever been. But to make that admission requires you to change your model and your staffing. It's far harder to run a business as a health business than as a residential business.'

Australia's residential aged-care sector, which looks after more than 200,000 people a year, is beyond broken. We have created a system where making money is more important than preserving life, where 'more' means operating with fewer staff, fewer of whom are on permanent contracts; a system that cuts corners and acts without empathy, without urgency; a system that disregards basic human dignity.

The royal commission heard that staff cuts had been ramped up during the pandemic and that many workers were struggling to access personal protective equipment, and that the government had no COVID-19 response plan for the sector. It also heard evidence of a 'frustrating level of dysfunction' between state and federal health authorities over whether to send infected residents to hospital and the failure of the Aged Care Quality and Safety Commission to adequately assess aged-care homes, instead relying on self-assessment surveys. At the most vulnerable time in their lives, we abandoned our elderly.

'The human misery and suffering must be acknowledged. This is the worst disaster that is still unfolding before my eyes and it's the worst in my entire career,' Professor Ibrahim told the royal commission. 'And what we've seen with COVID is that the system is broken at a high level because it's not the aged-care workers that have failed us in this. It is our people who are in governance roles—and I'm not even going to call them leaders because they're not leading—the people in governance positions who are accountable for what happens is where we have failed.'

What is the way forward? What must be done to fix the system? The Fridays for Future school strikes for climate-change action, spearheaded by Greta Thunberg, the ACT UP (AIDS Coalition to Unleash Power) group and the suffragette movement are all examples of highly functioning global grassroots campaigns that have created, or are creating, long-lasting change. Where are the people—on the national and international stage—advocating for the elderly and aged care?

'There is not a lobby group of ten people with dementia and Parkinson's disease who are on the street saying, "How dare you treat me this way." And if there was, they would die within two years,' Professor Ibrahim says. 'But there can't be any excuse for not changing [the status quo] when we know what the problem is. However, there is no one to push that change. There is literally no one.'

When he says no one, he means it.

'If my colleagues—who are in a privileged position, who can speak out and who are meant to represent the elderly, our patients, who were meant to advocate to the public—can't or won't do it, then who is going to do it?'

It is us, then, who must advocate for the elderly—for the elderly and the sick cannot be out on the streets themselves. We can advocate for a system that serves basic human rights, that is dignified, that is just, that is ethical. Much like the difficulties in garnering support for urgent climate-change action, the counterargument is all too often, *It is so far away, it won't happen to us*. But we are all ageing, and one day we will face difficult decisions about the ends of our lives, and those of our families and friends too, if we haven't already.

There are other mechanisms by which aged-care residents can be better represented. Just as the third chapter of this book advocated for an Indigenous voice to parliament, why couldn't aged-care residents also have representation in our political system? With an ageing population, the number of elderly Australians is only going to increase in coming decades.

'There are more than two hundred thousand of them, they deserve then to get a seat in the House of Representatives. There should be two people elected for them,' Professor Ibrahim says. Much like we must find ways for our Indigenous peoples' voices to be heard, we must find ways to enable society's most vulnerable to have a seat at the table.

Where neoliberalism has undermined the quality of aged care, paternalism has emerged as the way of managing the coronavirus response. 'We've had paternalistic doctors, predominantly male, leading the response. The people that run aged care, who actually do the doing, are predominantly nurses who are predominantly women,' Professor Ibrahim says. A sensible pandemic response would have put nurses front and centre, to tell the government, *This is how the place is run, this is how it works, this is how many casual staff we've got, and this is what we need to do*, rather than people who have no hands-on experience in aged care telling nurses how the sector works. 'The fundamental problem with aged care comes back to gender...Ninety per cent of the workforce is female and two-thirds of the [aged-care] population is female because men die younger,' Professor Ibrahim adds. 'Do you think aged care would be different if mostly men were in the homes? If you think it would be different and you can't explain why it would be different, but it would be, then I say to you there is a massive gender issue.' This pandemic has revealed that the impact of COVID-19 is starkly gendered, with the UN secretary-general António Guterres imploring governments to 'put women and girls at the centre of their efforts to recover from COVID-19. That starts with women as leaders, with equal representation and decision-making power.'

We do not know what the future of residential aged care will look like. The disaster may well send some of the major homes bankrupt. Some aged-care advocates, including Dr Sarah Russell, a public-health researcher who became passionate about the industry when her parents moved into a home, want the 1997 *Aged Care Act* to be rewritten from a human rights perspective:

> What is aged care for? Is it because older people are a great cohort to make money off? If that's the case, we keep the Act. If not, we rewrite it. It has to be written properly...We have to put older people front and centre, not the providers.

Russell would like to see transparency over staffing in facilities so families can make an informed decision on where to send their loved ones. While the royal commission's final report has not yet been published at the time of writing, in October 2020 it released a special report that made several recommendations. They include, among others, deploying infection control experts into nursing homes as a condition of accreditation and to 'ensure there are adequate staff available to allow continued visits to people living in residential aged care by their families and friends'.

Moving forward, Professor Ibrahim knows what he would like to see: a community-based model of care with adequately trained staff. 'What COVID-19 might do is...drive the model of care to be something quite different so we end up with much smaller housing, cluster-type houses for six to eight people. The homes that I've enjoyed visiting the most and that I think are good are the small community-run ones in regional areas where they look after the neighbours that they grew up with. Those ones have a real sense of community and social responsibility.' And there is certainly an appetite for it. Australians have signalled that they want more public money to be devoted to providing higher-quality aged care. And many have said in surveys that they are willing to pay higher taxes to fund it.

A REVOLUTION IN HEALTH

If there were ever a good time for a revolution to take place in a sector that has long been resistant to change, a pandemic is it. The health sector is notoriously old-school and conservative, reluctant to take up technology that might not only make doctors and other health-care workers' lives easier, but patients' too. So, when the federal government announced a sweeping expansion of telehealth services to reduce people's risk of exposure to COVID-19 and ensure uninterrupted access to care during lockdown, it was described as 'the most far-reaching change for general practice in a generation'.

Prior to the pandemic, doctors were able to claim Medicare Benefits Schedule (MBS) telehealth items for select services provided by phone or video call. The expansion during the pandemic enabled millions of Australians to access a wide range of health-care services safely from their homes, from a psychologist appointment to a medical abortion, whether they were five minutes away from the doctor or five hours. Marie Stopes Australia predicted that the pandemic would mean more women would need to be able to access abortion services from home and that domestic violence would increase. And they were right. At the height of the pandemic the organisation witnessed a 200 per cent increase in demand for medical abortion via telehealth compared with the previous year. It sent a very loud message: girls and women do not need to be in a clinic or a doctor's surgery to do medical abortion safely. 'What this pandemic has shown us is where we have big barriers in access to a whole range of services,' says Jacquie O'Brien, director of public affairs and policy at Marie Stopes Australia. 'Telehealth can't replace face-to-face [visits]—and nor should it—but women feel that it's convenient, that they're supported, that it's private. We also need to focus on people in rural and remote areas who simply can't get to a clinic because it's too far away and too expensive.'

With tens of thousands of Australians benefiting from the privilege of 'seeing' a health-care professional from the comfort of their home, it signals that the temporary expansion of telehealth services should be a permanent part of our health-care system. This is not just about protecting people from a virus; it is about providing alternative models of care that can reach more people.

With doctors, other health-care workers and patients on board—as well as influential bodies like the Australian Medical Association—we should also think beyond the scope of telehealth to ask: how else can we harness technology to improve our health-care sector? How can we make our health-care system more equitable, more accessible, more sustainable? We do not need to look far to see what is possible.

Sydney's Royal Prince Alfred Hospital is one of the country's busiest hospitals. A few months before the first case of COVID-19 was detected, plans were underway to transform it into an 'RPA Virtual' hospital. What began as a trial in February 2020 for palliative care and cystic fibrosis patients with just six nurses now has dozens more, as well as medical and allied health teams. Throughout the height of the pandemic, the hospital virtually cared for hundreds of COVID-19 patients who required follow-up but not a physical bed, thus freeing up beds for more urgent cases. The hospital—the first of its kind in the state—runs much like a regular hospital, with ward rounds, meetings and clinical handovers. The model has the potential to cut the number of unnecessary presentations at emergency departments, reduce the length of patients' stays in hospital and to empower patients, particularly those with chronic illnesses, to have a better quality of life. This new model of care helps us think about what sustainable, green health care can look like in the face of climate change. It also brings into focus the urgent need for reforms to reduce the waste and mitigate the harms caused by low-value interventions that provide little to no relief or benefit across both the public and private sectors. Invasive interventions with little proven benefit, such as colonoscopies for constipation or spinal fusion surgery for lower back pain, not only put people out of pocket but take up much-needed beds and staff time that could be used for people with greater care needs. For example, according to a study published in the *British Medical Journal*, in just one year almost 9000 low-value surgeries were done in public hospitals in NSW, at a cost of 30,000 hospital bed days that could have been put to better use.

The pandemic has also given momentum to the idea of expanding the scope of pharmacists' work to enable them to work alongside doctors in aged-care and primary-care settings, and to do more prescribing and management of patients, particularly those with chronic diseases such as diabetes. Nick Standen, pharmacist and lecturer in pharmacy at La Trobe University, says we can look to numerous countries that have expanded the role of pharmacists to include prescribing and vaccinating. 'Pharmacists are in a really good position to do these things, so why shouldn't they? From a professional and public-health standpoint, it makes sense for pharmacists to take on increased roles, but it's muddied by the fact that there's money involved and that's why it's a bit controversial,' he says. Controversy and the big pushback from doctors' groups aside, there are ongoing trials to allow pharmacists across Australia to prescribe an antibiotic for women with urinary tract infections. Most women experience a UTI at some point, and this system would allow them to quickly and easily access a low-risk drug without having to sit uncomfortably at a clinic waiting to see a doctor. It's a small example that nevertheless gives us pause to think about how our health-care system can be more integrated and how it can work better for us.

•••

The coronavirus pandemic has ground the entire apparatus of capitalism to a halt and exposed the toxic ramifications of a commitment to neoliberal ideology. Devotion to the free market has corroded our public services, reduced higher education to a factory of efficiency and productivity, increased inequality, and allowed the few to amass profits at the expense of casual and contract workers—and, ultimately, their lives. The fallout from the COVID-19 pandemic is a symptom of a much larger, systemic problem.

'Neoliberalism hasn't just undermined the quality of specific sectors like aged care and security but, by undermining the centrality of secure jobs that come with sick leave, career leave and annual leave, it has undermined the foundations of the modern welfare state that Australia spent the twentieth century building,' chief economist at the Australia Institute Richard Denniss writes in the *Guardian*.

The pandemic has exposed the deep-rooted inequalities that exist in our society. As we move towards an uncertain future, if we do not correct the course that we are on, we will head to an even darker place. But it is not too late to correct this course; there is hope. It is not too late to create a society that is founded on the principles of equality, fairness and justice. It is not too late to create a higher-education system that enshrines the principles upon which it was founded, nor is it too late to look after our elderly and the vulnerable with dignity and respect.

'As we pass through this portal into another kind of world, we will have to ask ourselves what we want to take with us and what we will leave behind,' writes author Arundhati Roy, in a piece about the COVID-19 pandemic. 'We may not always have a choice—but not thinking about it will not be an option.'

5 | CLIMATE CHANGE AND INDUSTRY

> 'You have stolen my dreams and my childhood with your empty words. And yet I'm one of the lucky ones. People are suffering. People are dying. Entire ecosystems are collapsing. We are in the beginning of a mass extinction, and all you can talk about is money and fairy tales of eternal economic growth. How dare you!'
>
> GRETA THUNBERG, 2019

A few days into 2020, Dr Michelle Hamrosi drove out to her general practice at Surf Beach, a small coastal town just south of Batemans Bay. She and her family had just spent six days away from their home, having evacuated under threat of fire. They camped at the back of a friend's shop in Batemans Bay as the fires raged all around, smoke plumes filling the scorched night sky. Michelle's children begged for their lives to return to normal. *This is our new normal*, she thought.

'There were so many fire fronts, and the behaviour of the fires was so unpredictable, that you felt like there wasn't anywhere safe to go,' she says. 'All the people in my community along the coast are all victims of climate change in a gross sort of way.'

The surgery had no power, phones or internet. Working by torchlight, Dr Hamrosi saw patients who were suffering from the symptoms of prolonged smoke exposure: difficulty breathing, sore eyes, hacking coughs. She heard stories of families desperately fleeing their homes, their children and animals in tow; stories of unspeakable loss, of not only ruined homes and possessions, but destroyed dreams and futures; stories of death, of the wildlife, bush, animals, all gone.

'I have three young kids and they have a vague idea of what is going on, but I don't want to scare them,' Dr Hamrosi says. 'I want them to have a rich childhood, but I'm worried about the future. We just had the worst fire season in history. What is in store for us?'

During our relentless Black Summer, I fly into Sydney to see my family. I look out the plane window to a barely recognisable harbour. The umber sun struggling to break through the curls of smoke reveals a bruised and bloody sky. Only days before, my mum had come to India for a visit, where she had snapped photos of New Delhi's air pollution, which left her both breathless and speechless. She gave me her face mask to hold onto until her next visit. She wouldn't need it back home in Australia, where she planned to soak up the clean air and enjoy balmy evenings on the deck.

Dozens of uncontrollable fires continue to burn across huge swathes of the country. People don't have the vocabulary to describe what is taking place. We resort to *apocalypse* over and over again, because that is exactly what it feels like. *Is this how the world ends*, I wonder.

The faces of our brave firefighters who leave behind families adorn nightly news bulletins. On New Year's Eve, army Blackhawk helicopters and navy ships are deployed to rescue thousands trapped on a beach after fire encircles the town of Mallacoota. Air quality in Canberra reaches twenty-two times the hazardous level set by the WHO. Western Sydney reaches 48.9 Celsius, making it the hottest place on Earth at the time. A haze of smoke blankets the continent. Dozens are dead. Thousands of homes and businesses burn to the ground, their remnants mere ash smouldering in the hot and humid wind. More than 18 million hectares of our unique flora and fauna burns. More than 800 million tonnes of carbon dioxide are emitted into the atmosphere. Over a billion animals burn to death.

As our country smouldered, Murdoch's News Corp, which comprises hundreds of local, national and international publishing outlets around the world, was more concerned with propagating misinformation to divert attention away from climate change. Over and over, the *Australian* newspaper argued that our Black Summer was no worse than those of the past.

'The country has never seen anything like it,' says scientist and conservationist Tim Flannery. 'The fires were so big, I mean, about twenty-one per cent of Australia's temperate broadleaf forests were burned during the season, the largest percentage ever burned in all recorded history, which before that was about two per cent. Given current levels of greenhouse gases in the atmosphere, we can expect a summer like last summer about once every eight years or less. Naturally they'd occur once every four hundred years.'

Despite the Australian Bureau of Meteorology confirming that 2019 was our hottest and driest year on record, the right-wing press decided that arson was responsible for the majority of fires. The *Herald Sun* and *Daily Telegraph* ran front-page spreads about the country's 'arson emergency' and the urgent need for an 'arson crackdown'. Scores of bots and trolls—many of which previously posted support for Donald Trump—amplified the Murdoch press's dangerous lie that Australia's fires were not the result of a 'climate emergency'. This, despite evidence that fewer than 1 per cent of the bushfires were started by arsonists.

The Murdoch media's attempt to legitimise climate-change denial is not new. Emeritus professor of politics and vice-chancellor's fellow at La Trobe University Robert Manne analysed 880 articles in the *Australian* newspaper between January 2004 and April 2011 and found that seven hundred were unfavourable to climate-change action. Of those, the majority were written by people lacking qualifications in any relevant discipline, let alone climate-change science.

As Australia faced its worst bushfire season ever, the prime minister was holidaying in Hawaii. His decision to post happy snaps of his family enjoying drinks by the beach as the country burned attracted a ferocious wave of anger that, as Judith Brett writes in her Quarterly Essay *The Coal Curse*, was totally misinterpreted.

'[Scott Morrison] thought this absence had made Australians anxious, as if he were a monarch whose very presence reassured and gave comfort,' she writes. 'What people wanted was not a hug from Scotty...they wanted him to talk about climate change, to admit that the ferocity and extent of these fires were what scientists had been predicting as the climate warmed.

'But Morrison will not admit to the severity of the crisis, nor that his government is failing to respond to its seriousness.'

How did Australia get here? How did climate-change scepticism—and denial—become so embedded among our supposed leaders?

The majority of climate-change deniers have never published in the field of climate change. As Robert Manne writes in the *Monthly*, 'Most but not all have no scientific education. And yet, somehow, they have come to believe that they understand better than the overwhelming majority of climate scientists...that the greenhouse-gas theory of global warming is "crap".'

'Climate-change denial has its strongest grip on aging white men, drawing on their need for certainty and control, the aggressive self-confidence they mobilise to defend these, and the projection of their own threatened sense of identity onto others,' Judith Brett writes in *The Coal Curse*.

It is the ageing white men who are threatened by the very fact that the world as they know it—one in which they've enjoyed domination, power and success—is in peril. When we combine ageing white men—the people who run our country—with neoliberal ideology, capitalism, vested economic interests and a powerful right-wing media, which amplifies the voices of climate denialists and fossil-fuel industry lobbyists over those of climate scientists, we have a toxic mix that threatens our very survival.

This is compounded by the fact that taking strong and effective action on climate change will require major disruption to life as we know it. To listen to the experts and take climate change seriously will mean fully embracing the need for massive economic change, which will require a completely new way of thinking.

But while many of us are busy greening our lives on the individual level—swapping cars for bicycles, installing solar panels on our roofs and giving up meat in favour of lentils—the corporate polluters are still out there, harming the atmosphere, our oceans and our land with impunity.

'The freedom of these corporations to pollute—and the fixation on a feeble lifestyle response—is no accident,' writes Martin Lukacs in the *Guardian*.

> It is result of an ideological war, waged over the last forty years, against the possibility of collective action… [Neoliberalism] tells you that you should not merely feel guilt and shame if you can't secure a good job, are deep in debt, and are too stressed or overworked for time with friends. You are now also responsible for bearing the burden of potential ecological collapse.

•••

At the end of 2019, as part of Australia was on fire, the world's governments met in Madrid under the United Nations Framework Convention on Climate Change for the twenty-fifth of its annual fortnight of meetings known as the Conference of the Parties (COP). While the world agreed to the Paris Agreement in 2015, the details of how countries would be held to account are still being worked out. Up for discussion at COP25 were a host of technical matters related to carbon markets, details on how poorer countries would be compensated for climate-related damage, and agreement on wording for how countries would ratchet up their efforts to reduce emissions by setting new benchmarks.

The talks didn't go as planned. Australia was accused of cheating, and was named and shamed as one of a handful of nations thwarting a deal on the 'rulebook' for the Paris Agreement. Alongside leaders like Donald Trump and Jair Bolsonaro, we were sidelined for our perceived indifference to the fires raging on our continent, in California and in the Amazon.

Before countries could agree to higher targets, though, the rules had to be figured out. Australia argued it should be allowed to use 'carryover credits' to reach its Paris targets from a different climate treaty. Federal energy minister Angus Taylor claimed Australia earned those credits by beating targets set out in the Kyoto Protocol. But the targets were woefully unambitious and had actually allowed Australia for a time to increase emissions. Many other countries had credits, but none planned on using them as a loophole to meet other targets. With carryover credits from Kyoto, Australia easily reaches its Paris target of a 26 per cent reduction in emissions from 2005 by 2030. Without them, we'd have to almost double our efforts to meet the target.

As the talks went beyond the allocated fourteen days and a stalemate set in, a decision on how to treat the credits was delayed until COP26, which was to be in held in Glasgow in 2020. COP26 has since been postponed due to another crisis linked to climate change: the COVID-19 pandemic.

'It is just cheating. Australia was willing in a way to destroy the whole system, because that is the way to destroy the whole Paris Agreement,' Laurence Tubiana, one of the architects of the agreement, said at the time. Her words were echoed by UN secretary-general António Guterres, who was left utterly demoralised by the conference's outcome: 'The international community lost an important opportunity to show increased ambition on mitigation, adaptation and finance to tackle the climate crisis.'

Australia's embarrassing performance on the global stage was even more disgraceful given that we were in the grips of what would become the most devastating fire season on record. And we had ignored the multiple warning signs. Numerous reports in the 1990s predicted that Australia's bushfire season in 2020 would be catastrophic. But according to Deputy Prime Minister Michael McCormack, those who linked bushfires to climate change were 'raving inner-city lunatics'.

Without wasting a second, Angus Taylor arrived back in Australia and immediately penned an opinion piece for the *Australian* arguing that we 'should be proud of our climate-change efforts'. What exactly were we to be proud of? In a 2019 international ranking of 57 countries, Australia was the worst performing country on climate-change policy. We do not even have a long-term national climate-change policy. But why would we need one? After all, Taylor wrote, since Australia is 'only' responsible for 1.3 per cent of global emissions, 'we can't single-handedly have a meaningful impact'.

Australia, which has just 0.3 per cent of the world's population, produces 1.3 per cent of world emissions. International targets, however, only take into account domestic emissions. Taylor purposely chose not to include emissions from the fossil fuels we export. When we add in coal and gas, we are responsible for 3.6 per cent of the world's emissions. China, India and the United States are the world's biggest emitters, but by taking population into account, these countries' levels pale in comparison. Per capita Australia in fact has the highest emissions in the OECD.

'Things have gone so pear-shaped in terms of our reduction of emissions,' says Matthew England, climate scientist and professor at the Climate Change Research Centre at UNSW. 'We've got a government right now who are completely blind to that risk.'

It is critical for us to understand the facts—not ones that can be shaped and twisted to fit a particular narrative that only serves to relieve a government of accountability and action. It is also critical that we explode the myth that climate change is an issue of the left or right. Climate change is a fact, not an ideology. Most Australians are savvy enough to believe that climate change is real; most of us are neither denialists nor sceptics. We agree on far more than we realise. But politics and the media polarise, so we are pitted against one another in a fictitious battle.

THE COST OF INACTION

Climate scientists—and writers of non-fiction and fiction—often like to talk about the year 2050. By then, the burden of greenhouse gases already existing in the atmosphere will have driven global average temperatures to around 1.5 degrees above pre-industrial levels. The Intergovernmental Panel on Climate Change, the UN's scientific body on climate change, warns that if we exceed 1.5 degrees of warming, the price we're paying right now for our inertia will pale in comparison.

The consequences of one-degree of warming are well known—we are living through it right now. It means catastrophic droughts, a rapid increase in the frequency and intensity of heatwaves, melting ice caps, increasing sea levels, disappearing islands, dwindling biodiversity, the mass displacement of people, and the global rise of the 'mega fire' that we have just lived through.

At 1.5 degrees of warming we can expect to lose up to 90 per cent of our reefs. The Great Barrier Reef will no longer exist. We can expect to see an ice-free Arctic summer once a century, mass food insecurity and the displacement of millions more people. We can expect cities to be washed away or abandoned. With the spread of climate change–related diseases, we can expect drastic declines in human health; we can expect mass species loss and catastrophic extinction.

There is far worse to come if we exceed 1.5 degrees of warming. A two-degree increase may push both human societies and natural ecosystems to the brink of survival. What lives and what dies? *Who* lives and who decides?

At current rates of global warming, it's projected we'll cross the 1.5-degree threshold between 2030 and 2052. And 1.5 degrees is the best case scenario. Currently, commitments made under the Paris Agreement are expected to increase global temperatures by around three degrees. The world as we know it would no longer exist. The IPCC says that to limit global warming to 1.5 degrees, we would need to have cut emissions by 45 per cent by 2030 (compared with 2010 levels) and bring them to net zero by 2050. That would mean a rapid, global push to abandon fossil-fuel use and remove carbon dioxide from the atmosphere.

'All the physical climate impacts—heat waves, droughts, bushfires, floods, sea-level rise, all these things, they affect Australia as bad as anywhere,' Professor England says. 'We've already sat here doing nothing for long enough that even though I'm saying the problems are thirty years from now, we're actually now thirty years from those first warnings. So, we're actually in the present tense. And the cost of climate change today far exceeds any of the costs of actually addressing the problem.'

Tim Flannery implores us to find a way to imagine the world as it will be decades from now—not just because it is our future, but also that of our children and grandchildren, whose lives will be affected by the decisions and actions that we take today. 'Many in the social sciences have given up on trying to imagine the future. Between the options of conceiving of it in present-day terms, plus the hyperbolic fantasy of much science fiction, perhaps their surrender is understandable,' he writes in his *Griffith Review* essay 'World in Motion'. 'Yet it is important that we find a way to envision the world as it will be decades from now.'

But it is difficult: we are not wired to make decisions about threats we struggle to imagine, in situations where the endpoint is uncertain. But to wait and see is to merely cling to the false hope that it won't be *that* bad if we maintain the status quo. This is not only deluded, it's unconscionable. To sleepwalk further into catastrophe, whether through credulous optimism or dangerous denial, would signal to future generations that we did not care. Climate change is not merely an environmental problem. It will be the defining moral issue of the twenty-first century. We all have a role to play. We all have something to lose.

...

Our Black Summer and the COVID-19 pandemic that followed taught us many things—one of which is that the human impulse to seek connection is indestructible. The flourishing of mutual aid throughout both crises evoked a sense of community beyond what we are accustomed to; it showed us that we are stronger together than we are apart, and that we can see ourselves as part of a collective. We are slowly waking up and realising that the immutable truths we understood as the basis of our social order are not rigid and inevitable, but constructions of our own making. They can be reshaped.

While COVID-19 presented immediate challenges of a different nature, it also made it impossible for us to ignore our ecological reality; it has allowed us to truly understand that we are not separate from or superior to our natural world. For many in lockdown in Australia, it brought a newfound appreciation for the environment, as we spent more time connecting with our immediate surroundings. We listened intentionally to the kookaburras laughing in the trees, and paid attention to the autumn leaves beneath our shoes. As cars, buses and trucks stopped clogging the roads, some people in the Indian Himalaya saw the mountains for the first time in their lives.

The pandemic has also shown us that we are adaptable, and capable of living completely different lives from the ones to which we are accustomed. It also showed us that drastic, far-reaching policy change can happen overnight. Our government put science above ideology, put human life above the economy, put experts, not politicians, at the centre of the response. Its response was far from perfect, but we can learn from it. If we can listen to the experts in a pandemic and take swift action to protect people, why can't we do the same for climate change? What if we approach chronic crises the same way as we approach immediate ones?

As Tim Flannery tells me, with both COVID-19 and climate change, we pre-commit to an outcome: that is, we establish the desired result and act in a way that will bring it about. So, for COVID-19 we committed to reducing the infection rate by shutting down the economy and locking down the nation, in the short term. Our medium-term issue then was to shore up the emergency capacity to deal with the crisis: do we have enough hospital beds? Do we have enough ventilators? Do we have enough contact tracers? The final phase is the search for a vaccine, to ensure we can live with the virus in the long term.

The same process applies to the threat of climate change, the only difference being the timeframe—what we do today will see results twenty or thirty years from now. To create a sustainable future, we must pre-commit to an outcome. That starts with drastically reducing our emissions. The next step is to ask questions: do we have the capacity to deal with the health effects of climate change? Heatwaves are Australia's largest natural killer. Do we have enough beds for that, and for smoke inhalation from fires? Can we save the Great Barrier Reef? 'In terms of climate change,' Flannery tells me, 'the vaccine is really drawdown; it's whether you can get enough gas out of the air to stabilise the climate system. The reason that's the equivalent of a vaccine is because of the pre-commitment. Right now, we're committed to a very bad outcome.'

If we think of the timeline of climate change in terms of that of COVID-19, he says, that would put us in mid-March 2020—the last possible moment for emergency action.

A GREEN RECOVERY

Around the world, countries are seizing the once-in-a-lifetime opportunity the pandemic provides to move towards zero emissions by implementing a range of green recovery programs. The global call for a green recovery has been heralded by climate activists and conservationists, but also by energy companies, banks, investors and industry. The idea has been supported by governments from Canada to Pakistan. The German government, for example, has called for recovery programs to invest in future-proof jobs that contribute towards cutting emissions.

In Australia, the National COVID-19 Coordination Commission was created to help steer the government's economic and social recovery from the pandemic. It's headed by Nev Power, the former head of iron ore miner Fortescue Metals, who is now a director and major shareholder of oil and gas company Strike Energy. Until September 2020, other members also included Catherine Tanna, managing director of EnergyAustralia, one of the country's leading gas retailers, and Andrew Liveris, a board member of Aramco, a major Saudi oil company.

The commission, which did not use an independent appointment process to select its members, has lacked transparency since its inception in March. In September, the *Guardian* revealed that the taskforce also received 'pro bono' advice from a lobbying firm with links to the Saudi government and gas companies. The University of Melbourne wrote a scathing policy brief on the government's COVID-19 commission, which it called an 'enduring risk to Australian democracy' that must be overhauled. The body has called for $6 billion of investment in gas development in Australia. Natural gas is the fastest growing source of carbon dioxide in the atmosphere as the global push away from coal intensifies.

'This is a terrible idea,' writes Samantha Hepburn, director of the Centre for Energy and Natural Resources Law at Deakin University, in the *Conversation*. 'Spending billions on gas infrastructure and development under the guise of a COVID-19 economic recovery strategy—with no attempt to address pricing or anti-competitive behaviour—is ill-considered and injudicious.'

How does it make sense—environmentally and economically—to invest in gas when renewable energy and storage solutions are expanding at such a fast pace? How could anyone—except those who stand to benefit—believe this is a wise idea?

'We're so in need of reductions in emissions, we cannot step from one fossil fuel to another,' Professor England says. 'It should not be on our radar for our future—it's a greenhouse gas.'

In 2017, when Scott Morrison was the treasurer, he walked into the House of Representatives clutching a lump of black coal. 'This is coal,' he said, brandishing the chunk as if were a trophy. 'Don't be afraid, don't be scared.' The lump was intended as a symbol of how the federal government was going to keep the lights on, keep power prices low and, most importantly, protect jobs. It was a stunt designed to paint Labor as caring so little about the coal-worker electorate that they would pursue green energy under the banner of action on climate change and destroy their livelihood.

Judith Brett's *The Coal Curse* traces the history of Australia as a trading nation to examine how we got to where we are today. In the 1990s, as the global coal rush, spurred on by China and India, was getting underway, climate scientists were demanding the burning of fossils be urgently and drastically reduced. Angered by the damning science and growing calls to curb emissions, she writes, the fossil-fuel industry needed to quickly find a way to prevent the federal government from signing international agreements committing to carbon-emissions reductions. It had to find a powerful narrative against bipartisan climate-change action. What better than to frame the issue as one of the environment versus jobs? It was an easy argument to win. If you took steps to reduce emissions, thousands of hardworking Australians would be destitute and our economy would flounder.

'Their core argument was that mining underpinned Australia's wealth, so policies that reduced carbon emissions would damage the whole economy,' Brett writes. Industry also took the opportunity to cement climate scepticism in the minds of the powerful.

Lobbying, advocacy and political donations are completely legal in Australia. But the fossil-fuel industry has gone far beyond this—to what Brett describes as 'state capture', in which private interest has been allowed to shape government decisions for gain. Brett cites as telling evidence the lack of government policymaking access given to environmental and community groups that oppose the expansion of mining. We can now add the National COVID-19 Coordination Commission's lack of transparency to the list. 'In making climate policy, the Australian federal government has not listened to the arguments of all interested groups as if it were a neutral umpire, because it was already captured by advocates of fossil fuels,' she writes. 'This is the political face of the resource curse.'

The fossil-fuel industry has a stranglehold on government policy and too many people are reaping the benefits for there to be sufficient motivation to stop polluting the planet. 'The fossil-fuel sectors turn up in Canberra and they have very good relationships with politicians,' Professor England says. 'The government likes the money it can get as well—and they take a cut of it, of course. This has created a culture here where basically the narrative is that we can't address climate change because we're a small part of the problem and we put jobs ahead of the environment. The irony is that the jobs that are created by solving this problem far exceed the jobs in mining. The coal industry employs fewer people than Bunnings Warehouse.'

Coalmining employs just over 35,000 people—ten thousand fewer people than the car industry, which former Coalition prime minister Tony Abbott allowed to shut down. Mining overall makes up 1.9 per cent of the workforce. Australia's top three exports are iron ore, coal and natural gas. We are the world's largest exporter of coal and the world's second-largest exporter of gas. This makes us the world's third-largest exporter of fossil fuels, behind Russia and Saudi Arabia. So almost 70 per cent of our export income is derived from just 4.4 per cent of the workforce. 'We are still a country that depends overwhelmingly on the export of a few primary commodities shipped to the world raw and requiring very few of us to produce,' Brett writes.

This means there is a huge disconnect between the section of the economy that earns most of the export income and the one that creates most of the jobs. It wasn't always this way. There was a time when Australia manufactured a huge array of goods—from cars and washing machines to footwear and fridges. Manufacturing used to be a significant percentage of our GDP and at its height it employed almost a third of the workforce, as Brett highlights. The Second World War had a major impact on Australian manufacturing, as we thrived off migration, protectionist tariffs and foreign investment. But as time went on, the tariffs proved a double-edged sword, as we created an economy where consumers could buy Australian goods—but at a cost far greater than if they were imported from Asian countries that now had thriving manufacturing industries. Throughout the 1980s and 1990s, as Australia's economy underwent huge economic reform, major tariff cuts were implemented, which saw us go from having one of the most protected manufacturing industries in the world to the least. The few industries like textiles and clothing that thought they could survive simply couldn't compete with China. The neoliberal agenda, as Brett writes, 'marked the end of Australia's long-held aspiration to be a modern industrial nation...We are no longer a country that makes much.' Today, manufacturing makes up less than 6 per cent of our GDP.

The pandemic has, with great speed, made us acutely aware of how little we make. As recently as a decade ago, most trains were designed and manufactured here. That is no longer the case. The car manufacturing industry is dead. And when the pandemic hit, we only had one manufacturer of surgical masks. International shortages—along with restrictions—on the export of medical equipment and personal protective equipment gave us pause to realise how dependent we are on global trade. When we have only one company manufacturing surgical masks in Australia, we have to ask: what would happen in the event of another pandemic, or war, or ecological calamity? Would we have the ability to look after ourselves?

'Australia needs to be more self-reliant, and what we have done as a nation is that we've become really, really efficient at certain things,' ANU vice-chancellor Brian Schmidt says. 'And unless you have real visionary people who aren't mercantile in their approach to politics and to policy, you're going to end up as a less well-off nation to the point where you eventually become a banana republic.'

Australia is at a crossroads. Our manufacturing industry is weak, we are heavily reliant on producing fossil fuels for export—an industry that does not employ many people—and the world is rapidly moving away from coal. What happens when (not if) countries divest fully from fossil fuels? In a sign of things to come, China has already said it will reach carbon neutrality before 2060. If we do not embrace alternatives, we have a major economic problem. And this is true whether or not you believe in climate change. The economic tides are for alternative energy.

The pandemic has provided us with an extraordinary opportunity to build a carbon-free, green economy, to move away from fossil fuels, to rebuild a manufacturing presence on the back of large-scale renewable energy, and to create a safe future for coming generations. It will require a massive shake-up, but we know that it is possible—if we so choose. We *can* manufacture a new Australian dream.

'If you are thinking about COVID-19 and a COVID-19 economic stimulus, we shouldn't be doing anything that's inconsistent with a low-emissions future,' says Tony Wood, director of the Grattan

Institute's energy program. 'I do not believe in a gas-led recovery. I actually believe in a renewables-led recovery. Now is the time.'

...

What would a renewables-led recovery look like? How could we get there? In his book *Superpower: Australia's Low-Carbon Opportunity*, economist Ross Garnaut describes how if Australia rises to the challenge of climate change it will emerge as a global superpower in energy, low-carbon industry and absorption of carbon in the landscape. 'If we take early and strong action in ways that build upon our natural advantages, we will not suffer a decline in living standards in the near future in conventional economic terms as we move towards zero emissions,' he writes. 'Now, much more than was anticipated a decade ago, we can be confident that we will be richer materially sooner rather than later, as well as very much richer in human and natural heritage, should we embrace a zero-emissions future.' He points to two sources that will make it possible.

One is our climate, which gives us a huge natural advantage in the production of renewable energy. We have unusually high levels of sun for the production of solar energy; we also have significant wind resources. As Tony Wood tells me, our natural resources for renewable energy are so impressive that on a per capita basis, we are superior to every other country on the planet. In addition to this advantage, we have a small domestic economy and a comparatively small population. With a rapid fall in the cost of solar and wind energy, rather than shipping raw minerals off to faraway places only to import them back again, we can produce them here.

Secondly, according to Garnaut, is 'the immense opportunity for capturing and sequestering, at relatively low cost, atmospheric carbon in soils, pastures, woodlands, forest and plantations'. This means, he writes, that Australia should therefore have a stronger comparative advantage in the zero-emissions world economy than it did in the 'fossil-energy past'.

Looking ahead, one of the most exciting opportunities, Wood says, is in creating a green steel industry. Currently, Australia ships most of its raw iron ore and metallurgical coal used in steel production to Asian countries, where it is processed. Steel contributes 7 per cent to global emissions. Green steel is created using hydrogen to strip the oxygen out of iron ore. The metal is then refined into steel. Wood says that green steel made with renewable hydrogen could become a major export industry employing up to 25,000 people in the coal-mining regions likely to be hardest hit by global efforts to cut emissions, such as the Hunter Valley in NSW, and central Queensland. Pilot green steel plants have been built in Sweden and Germany, while the global car industry has already signalled that it wants to move to zero-emissions cars—and those will require green steel.

'When you look at it, we could seriously rebuild Australia's steel manufacturing sector in a way that would be dramatic,' Wood says. 'The economics favour it, it will create jobs, it will politically be very important if we are ever going to have a useful climate-change policy and it would potentially replace for Australia the export revenue that we currently get from all the metallurgical coal that the world is going to turn away from anyway. Because of our current dependence upon carbon-intensive manufacturing, carbon-intensive extraction or industries, we have a lot of people who were trained in skillsets and trades that are similar to what you would need in the steelmaking business. We also have a lot of infrastructure—we have the ports and we have the electricity grid.'

Australia could also expand its production of aluminium, silicon and ammonia, Wood says. Ammonia, for example, is made in Newcastle and Gladstone, and is used to produce global supplies of explosives and fertilisers. If gas were replaced with renewable hydrogen, which is produced through electrolysis using renewable electricity and which is increasingly being seen as a viable alternative to liquid natural gas, production would have zero emissions. This also poses the opportunity for Australia to become a primary producer of renewable hydrogen in the future. While hydrogen is usually used in the manufacture of glass, steel and fertiliser, the greatest demand for it in the future will likely come from its use as a fuel—for hydrogen-powered electric cars and public transport. We would not make the cars ourselves, but we could position ourselves as a major exporter.

Meanwhile, according to Simon Holmes à Court, a senior adviser to the Climate and Energy College at the University of Melbourne, our shaky aluminium industry could be given a major boost if our four aluminium smelters, which use a huge percentage of electricity from the grid, were made more flexible. He wants to upgrade the smelters 'so they add value to the grid just as they add value to the communities in which they operate'. That would be done by retrofitting them with a 'virtual battery', allowing them to turn up or turn down the amount of energy they consume.

Aside from the Grattan Institute, there are a growing number of organisations working on what a green recovery could look like for Australia. Beyond Zero Emissions, a non-profit climate-change solutions think tank, has developed a 'million jobs plan' that envisions a low-carbon recovery from COVID-19 which in the space of five years would create up to 1.8 million jobs. It says, for example, there could be up to 200,000 new jobs in renewable energy, 900,000 new jobs in net-zero energy buildings, 140,000 jobs in modernising our manufacturing industry and 75,000 jobs in renewable mining—70 per cent of which would be in regional areas. The think tank, which is working with Ross Garnaut, believes that a deep energy retrofit would improve the efficiency of three million buildings so they no longer have to pay electricity bills, while transport could run on clean power and our recycling system could be fixed so 100 per cent of materials are recovered.

The Greens, meanwhile, have come out in support of building Australia's green steel and aluminium industry, and want to see Australia be running on 100 per cent renewable energy by 2030. This could be achieved by building the necessary infrastructure and prioritising the construction of the publicly owned transmission network.

Garnaut believes Australia could have an affordable, clean electricity system running at more than three times its existing capacity, which would power a transformed economy. As he writes, if Australia is to realise its opportunity in a zero-carbon world economy, it will require a fundamentally different policy framework. But, he says, 'the advantages of the low-carbon world are so great for Australia that we can make a strong start even with incomplete and weak policies... Policies to support the completion of the transition can be built in a political environment that has been changed by early success.' We can look to Queensland as an example. The state has announced a $500 million renewable energy fund to build publicly owned wind and solar projects as a key part of its post-pandemic recovery plan.

Professor England compares the opportunity provided by the pandemic to decarbonise the economy and take action on reducing emissions to the economic growth that took place following the

Second World War. 'I call it a warlike effort, by which I mean that it's an effort where you mobilise all possible resources and new infrastructure around decarbonising the economy,' he says. 'The irony in all this is that the amount of money that has been thrown at this pandemic is way more than we ever needed to solve climate change. Governments have been prepared to go into debt over the pandemic, but they should have been prepared to go into debt over climate change.'

• • •

Bob Vickers is a young doctor who grew up in the Upper Hunter Valley, one of Australia's major wine regions. It's also one of our major coalmining areas. Open-cut mines spread across the valley from Newcastle to Muswellbrook. He suffered asthma throughout his childhood—as almost one in five kids in the region do today—and now as a doctor he is witnessing the devastating health impacts of air pollution on his patients.

For the first time, in 2020, Greenpeace assessed the health impacts of burning coal for electricity on the population. Australia still operates twenty-two coal-burning power stations, which are among the oldest and dirtiest in the world. The organisation found that air pollution from the ageing coal-fired power stations spreads hundreds of kilometres from regional plants into major cities and kills around eight hundred people each year. On average, each year the pollution causes 850 babies to be born with low birth weight, which puts them at greater risk of serious health conditions like heart disease and diabetes, and at least fourteen thousand asthma attacks among children.

Dr Vickers says the two different types of particles of pollution that are emitted—coarse and fine particles—can also cause other respiratory diseases, miscarriage, strokes, stillbirths and neonatal deaths. 'There's this real attitude that it's just dust and if you don't like it you can just move. It is not just dust. It's particle pollution and you're breathing it in,' he says. 'Clean air is a basic human right. The health impacts of climate change are just innumerable.'

Power stations in Australia are licensed to emit pollutant concentrations that dramatically exceed limits set by comparable countries, including across Europe. Air-quality monitoring in the region regularly shows results that not only drastically exceed international limits but even own our national standards. Last year, for example, the Hunter Valley region had over a thousand alerts where the twenty-four-hour average of air pollution exceeded the recommended national standard. 'The power stations could be upgraded for a fraction of the profit they make each year, but they don't have to because no one is forcing them to do it,' Dr Vickers says.

He echoes the Grattan Institute and Beyond Zero Emissions, among a growing number of organisations, in calling for a renewable-led pandemic recovery program. 'The Hunter Valley has the ability to be something much better going forward. We have a rail line all the way to the country's largest export port in Newcastle. We have a workforce of welders, boilermakers, electricians, heavy-vehicle operators. We could transform the region into a green manufacturing and circular manufacturing hub. Coal is not going to be here forever. I want to fix this problem—I do not want to just walk away.'

•••

In July 2020, Katta O'Donnell, a law student at La Trobe University, launched a legal action against the Australian government. The twenty-three-year-old is suing the federal government, arguing that in issuing sovereign bonds, it has failed to disclose the financial risks associated with climate change. The case, which is a world first on this specific allegation, is not without precedent. In 2015, a Dutch environmental group, the Urgenda Foundation, and almost nine hundred Dutch citizens sued the Dutch government, saying it had a legal duty to prevent climate change. 'Judicial intervention is now our only hope of averting dangerous climate change,' Dutch lawyer Roger Cox said at the time. In a historic win, the Hague ruled the government must cut its greenhouse emissions by at least 25 per cent by the end of 2020 (compared to 1990 levels), concluding that because of the 'severity of the consequences', the state has a duty to take climate-change mitigation measures.

Two months after O'Donnell, and in yet another Australian first, a class action was launched on behalf of young people across the globe, which seeks an injunction to stop the federal government approving an extension to Whitehaven's Vickery coal mine in north-west NSW. The class action argues that digging up and burning coal will further harm young people by exacerbating climate change. There are eight representative plaintiffs, who are all teenagers, many of whom met during School Strike for Climate, also known as Fridays for Future. If the case is successful, it could spell major problems for any new coalmine in Australia—and possibly other fossil-fuel projects. The consequences could reverberate around the world.

This new wave of climate litigation—led by our youth—should serve as a catalytic reminder of what is at stake. Those most vulnerable to both the direct and indirect consequences of climate change are children and youth. The WHO estimates that children will suffer more than 80 per cent of the illnesses, injuries and deaths attributable to climate change. We now have teenagers fighting for their future in the court of law. They are radical for the very fact that they have no other choice. Their silence is not an option.

Toby Thorpe is from Tasmania and has been a climate activist since he was twelve. At eighteen years old, he is now the executive director of the Climate Justice Initiative, and wants us to view climate change through the lens of social justice. Today's youth, he says, understand better than any other generation what the concepts of equity, justice and fairness mean. 'Youth understand the role we can play in changing the world because we have the most to lose. The pandemic has really projected that youth voice onto the frontline to ask: what is my government doing to support me and my future? We have to recognise that the consequences of climate change are a result of a failed system and that failed system is so important to understand. When we look at the Black Lives Matter movement, poverty, food security, gender, LGBTQI, all these things are the side effects of not achieving justice and what they have in common is climate change. Why is that blanket being added to the earth? It comes back to the social issue of how the emissions got into the atmosphere in the first place. Every emission has a social element.'

Ross Garnaut echoes his thoughts, writing in *Superpower: Australia's Low-Carbon Opportunity*, 'Each tonne of greenhouse-gas emissions is reasonably expected to impose some extra damage on someone, somewhere. That the victim is unknown does not diminish the responsibility. This personal ethical obligation is in addition to our responsibility as citizens to work for the introduction and implementation of policies that achieve good climate outcomes.'

A VOTE FOR CHANGE

At the 2019 election, former prime minister and climate-change denier Tony Abbott lost his Warringah seat—a conservative stronghold—in a landslide. He lost to independent Zali Steggall who ran on a platform of climate-change action. Independent Helen Haines, another campaigner for climate-change action, succeeded fellow independent Cathy McGowan to the seat of Indi in Victoria, the first time in Australian political history that a seat was won by an independent two times in a row. The Grattan Institute's 2018 report 'A Crisis of Trust' found that since 2007 the share of votes for minor parties and independents has skyrocketed—and shows no sign of abating.

Just before lockdown, hundreds of people attended a meeting in Sydney's south with the aim of ousting their local member, climate-change denier-in-chief Craig Kelly. The Liberal federal member for Hughes has spent a decade in parliament campaigning against climate-change science. His social media is littered with comments such as 'Bushfires have nothing to do with "climate change"' and 'Beware of climate alarmists: Everything they tell you is a lie.' Locals in the Sutherland Shire desperately want to replace him with a representative who understands not only that climate change is real, but that it requires action—and quickly. They have now formed a group called 'We Are Hughes' and are campaigning for the electorate to be represented by someone who believes in evidence-based facts. A climate-change denier doesn't cut it.

What the rise in support for independents and the community political processes they use suggests is that the Australian electorate is yearning for more opportunities to be involved in the debate. We want to be heard; we want to be listened to.

Tim Flannery hypothesises what type of government we'd have today if more independents had succeeded in 2019. 'We could have a different government right now, which would be being held to the grindstone to deal with climate change,' he says. 'You've got to get people to vote on the issue, that is the thing that will change the politics [of climate change]. While we have a corrupt government that's ignoring the issue, we can do very little because we can't get the emergency response we need. As a matter of urgency, in the next couple of years, we need to get rid of the coal-fired power plants, implement a good electric-vehicle policy, go to the global meetings with a very aggressive carbon abatement project, seek to join the Europeans on carbon tariffs, and it will make a difference.'

Thorpe, who is just old enough to vote, agrees. He believes that creating a nurturing environment that enables young people to take part in politics is the key to galvanising long-lasting climate-change action. 'We have the capacity and capability [to combat climate change] but politics is the huge barrier to that optimism becoming a practicality. So many young people are so politically minded, and we need to get them elected. Just putting your name on a ballot creates such a difference; putting your hand up to say, "I am going to run because this electorate doesn't represent the views of young people" is so powerful,' he says.

In a free and fair democracy—where we are not just afforded the right to vote, but required to—arguably the greatest, most powerful thing that we can do on an individual level is voting for representatives who will take action on climate change. We can add solar roofs to our homes, reduce our consumption, swap meat for pulses, give up our cars for public transport—all of which are all excellent things to do. But the most meaningful thing we can do is vote. Vote for change. Vote for action. Vote for people who represent our beliefs.

The pandemic has exposed some of the lies we were led to believe about why governments cannot act. We know we *can* take action on climate change—if we so choose. We know we can make sweeping changes to policy overnight. We know that we *can* put human life over the economy. We know that taking action on climate change will not decimate the economy. We know that taking action on climate change will create jobs. We know that the government can take extraordinary steps to protect us—if it so chooses. We know that the cost of inaction will be devastating.

•••

The pandemic has, with great speed, fundamentally altered the world in which we live. The changes it has wrought are of a type and on a scale unseen by most people alive. It has challenged the truths we believed to be absolute and shown us they are constructions of our own making. We can reshape them. By the time you read this, we may have a vaccine against COVID-19. We may not. A vaccine will likely be a panacea for a country as privileged as Australia. People will not be left behind because of gender, race, ethnicity, disability, sexual orientation, socio-economic status, class, caste or religion. But a vaccine will not take us back to the old world. That world is gone. We now have to decide on the new principles and values that will underpin our society as we move forward. We bear a huge responsibility.

What do we want to take with us from the old world? What do we want to leave behind? This is a time of reawakening and resurrection. It is a time for reflection and readjustment. It is an opportunity to build something better on the back of what we know—for all of us now and for the generations to come.

Throughout this book I have examined how we can create a better, more just, more equal Australia. I have explored what that Australia would look like and how we could create it. Climate change is the natural end to this story. It is connected to every topic, every issue this book has touched on—and many, many more. It is the greatest moral challenge of our time.

It is clear that neoliberalism and capitalism are incompatible with humans living in peace with the Earth. The very fact that the wealthiest 1 per cent of the world's population are responsible for the emission of more than twice as much carbon dioxide as the poorest 50 per cent of the world should alleviate any lingering beliefs that our economic systems are fit for purpose. But the good news is that this concentration of wealth and power is ever more visible. People are starting to realise what is wrong and how we can fix it.

Moving forward, 'We need to fundamentally re-evaluate our relationship to ownership, work and capital,' as Phil McDuff writes in the *Guardian*. We also need to undertake a dramatic reconfiguration of our industrial economy, while at the same time creating a welfare system that will enable and facilitate the changes we need to make. And we need to build institutions that reflect our values of fairness, inclusion, equality, justice, reciprocity. They will not give everyone a voice, but they will empower us all. Last but not least, we need to drastically cut our greenhouse-gas emissions, embrace the clean alternatives and create a thriving carbon-free economy. We need to refigure our relationship to and with the environment.

I do not know what the future holds, but I do know we are at a critical juncture in history. Whatever path we choose to take in the wake of the pandemic will not only define the lives of generations of Australians to come but the future of our planet. Every Australian has a role to play in first imagining, and then creating, the type of society, country and world that we want to be a part of. It is this collective vision—of a better and brighter future—that fills me with so much hope.

WORKS CITED

INTRODUCTION

Birch, Kean. 'What Exactly Is Neoliberalism?'. *Conversation*. 3 November 2017. theconversation.com/what-exactly-is-neoliberalism-84755

Flanagan, Richard. 'Did the Coronavirus Kill Ideology in Australia?'. *New York Times*. 18 May 2020. nytimes.com/2020/05/18/opinion/coronavirus-australia.html

1. GOVERNMENT AND POLITICS

Beem, Christopher. *The Necessity of Politics: Reclaiming American Public Life*. University of Chicago Press, United States. 1999.

Caldwell, Louise. 'I Took Part in a Citizens' Assembly—It Could Help Break the Brexit Deadlock'. *Guardian*. 16 January 2019. theguardian.com/commentisfree/2019/jan/16/citizens-assembly-ireland-abortion-referendum

City of Melbourne. Participate Melbourne. 2014. participate.melbourne.vic.gov.au/10yearplan

City of Sydney. Planning for Sydney 2050—Have Your Say, 2019. cityofsydney.nsw.gov.au/vision-setting/planning-sydney-2050-have-your-say

Cox, Eva. *A Truly Civil Society: Boyer Lecture Series*. ABC Books, Australia. 1995.

Democracy 2025. democracy2025.gov.au

Denniss, Richard. *Dead Right: How Neoliberalism Ate Itself and What Came Next*. Black Inc., Australia. 2018.

Dunlop, Tim. *The Future of Everything: Big, Audacious Ideas for a Better World*. NewSouth Publishing, Australia. 2018.

Hollo, Tim. 'Australians' Faith in Politics Has Collapsed—How Can We Reimagine Democracy?'. *Guardian*. 19 July 2019. theguardian.com/australia-news/commentisfree/2019/jul/19/australians-faith-in-politics-has-collapsed-how-can-we-reimagine-democracy

Luu, Chi. 'Towards a Reconception of Power: Modernising Our Magical Thinking'. *Griffith Review 67: Matters of Trust*. 2020. griffithreview.com/articles/towards-a-reconception-of-power

Moore, Frances et al. 'Rapidly Declining Remarkability of Temperature Anomalies May Obscure Public Perception of Climate Change'. *Proceedings of the National Academy of Sciences of the United States of America*, 116(11). February 2019.

Putnam, Robert. *Bowling Alone: The Collapse and Revival of American Community*. Simon & Schuster, United States. 2000.

Scheidel, Walter. *The Great Leveller: Violence and the History of Inequality from the Stone Age to the Twenty-First Century*. Princeton University Press, United States. 2017.

South Australian Government. Nuclear Fuel Cycle Royal Commission. 2015. nuclearrc.sa.gov.au

Tiernan, Anne. 'Active Citizens, Constructive Answers: Taking Control of the Processes of Democracy'. *Griffith Review 67: Matters of Trust*. 2020. griffithreview.com/articles/active-citizens-constructive-answers

Voices for Indi. voicesforindi.com/about/reports

Wood, Tony et al. 'A Crisis of Trust: The Rise of Protest Politics in Australia'. Grattan Institute Report No. 2018–05. March 2018. grattan.edu.au/report/a-crisis-of-trust

2. WELFARE

Basic Income Earth Network. basicincome.org

Bregman, Rutger. *Utopia for Realists: And How We Can Get There*. Bloomsbury Publishing, United Kingdom. 2014.

Committee for Economic Development of Australia. 'Australia's Future Workforce?'. June 2015. ceda.com.au/CEDA/media/ResearchCatalogueDocuments/Research%20and%20Policy/PDF/26792-Futureworkforce_June2015.pdf

Denniss, Richard. *Dead Right: How Neoliberalism Ate Itself and What Came Next*. Black Inc., Australia. 2018.

Dunlop, Tim. *Why the Future Is Workless*. NewSouth Publishing, Australia. 2016.

Dunlop, Tim. *The Future of Everything: Big, Audacious Ideas for a Better World*. NewSouth Publishing, Australia. 2018.

Flanagan, Richard. 'Did the Coronavirus Kill Ideology in Australia?'. *New York Times*. 18 May 2020. nytimes.com/2020/05/18/opinion/coronavirus-australia.html

The Green Institute. 'Views of a Universal Basic Income: Perspectives Across Australia'. 2017. greeninstitute.org.au/wp-content/uploads/2017/06/Views_of_a_UBI_Aust.pdf

Huntley, Rebecca. *Still Lucky: Why You Should Feel Optimistic about Australia and Its People*. Penguin Group Australia. 2017.

Klein, E. et al. *Implementing a Basic Income in Australia: Pathways Forward.* Palgrave Macmillan, Australia. 2019.

Klein, Naomi. *This Changes Everything: Capitalism vs. the Climate*. Simon & Schuster, United States. 2014.

Lewis, Simon L. & Maslin, Mark A. *The Human Planet: How We Created the Anthropocene*. Yale University Press, United States. 2018

Miller, Claire Cain. 'Nearly Half of Men Say They Do Most of the Home Schooling. 3 Per Cent of Women Agree'. *New York Times*. 6 May 2020. nytimes.com/2020/05/06/upshot/pandemic-chores-homeschooling-gender.html

Services Australia. servicesaustralia.gov.au/individuals/subjects/payments-and-services-during-coronavirus-covid-19

Standing, Guy. 'India's Experiment in Basic Income Grants', *Global Dialogue*, 3(5). 2013.

Tiernan, Anne. 'Active Citizens, Constructive Answers: Taking Control of the Processes of Democracy'. *Griffith Review 67: Matters of Trust*. 2020. griffithreview.com/articles/active-citizens-constructive-answers

Quiggin, John. johnquiggin.com

Australian Council of Social Service, in partnership with the University of NSW. 'Inequality in Australia 2018'. 2019. events.unsw.edu.au/sites/default/files/2019-01/Inequality-in-Australia-2018_0.pdf

3. INDIGENOUS AFFAIRS

Australian Bureau of Statistics. *Causes of Death, Australia, 2009*. abs.gov.au/ausstats/abs@.nsf/Products/4FCC60392960B1AECA25788400127B9D?opendocument

Centers for Disease Control and Prevention. *History of 1918 Flu Pandemic*. cdc.gov/flu/pandemic-resources/1918-commemoration/1918-pandemic-history.htm

Commonwealth of Australia, Department of Health. Aboriginal and Torres Strait Islander Advisory Group on Covid-19. health.gov.au/committees-and-groups/aboriginal-and-torres-strait-islander-advisory-group-on-covid-19

Commonwealth of Australia. *Closing the Gap in Partnership*. closingthegap.gov.au/national-agreement-closing-gap-glance

Commonwealth of Australia, Department of the Prime Minister and Cabinet. *Closing the Gap Report 2020*. ctgreport.niaa.gov.au

Davis, Megan. 'The Long Road to Uluru'. *Griffith Review 60: First Things First*. 2018. griffithreview.com/articles/long-road-uluru-walking-together-truth-before-justice-megan-davis

Davis, Megan. 'New Agreement Won't Deliver the Change Indigenous Australians Need'. *Sydney Morning Herald*. 8 July 2020. smh.com.au/national/new-agreement-won-t-deliver-the-change-indigenous-australians-need-20200705-p5593d.html

Davis, Megan. 'Reconciliation and the Promise of an Australian Homecoming. *Monthly*. July 2020. themonthly.com.au/issue/2020/july/1593525600/megan-davis/reconciliation-and-promise-australian-homecoming

Farmer, Paul. *Infections and Inequalities: The Modern Plagues*. University of California Press, United States. 2001.

Karp, Paul. 'Ken Wyatt Concedes Referendum on Indigenous Recognition Unlikely Before Election'. *Guardian*. 29 May 2020. theguardian.com/australia-news/2020/may/29/ken-wyatt-concedes-referendum-on-indigenous-recognition-unlikely-before-election

KPMG. 'Maranguka Justice Reinvestment Project: Impact Assessment'. 27 November 2018. justreinvest.org.au/wp-content/uploads/2018/11/Maranguka-Justice-Reinvestment-Project-KPMG-Impact-Assessment-FINAL-REPORT.pdf

Mayor, Thomas. *Finding the Heart of the Nation: The Journey of the Uluru Statement towards Voice, Treaty and Truth*. Hardie Grant Travel, Australia. 2019.

McQuire, Amy. 'We Must Bear Witness to Black Deaths in Our Own Country'. *Canberra Times*. 31 May 2020. canberratimes.com.au/story/6775418/we-must-bear-witness-to-black-deaths-in-our-own-country

McQuire, Amy. 'Aboriginal Community Health's Success with COVID-19'. *Saturday Paper*. 25 April–1 May 2020. thesaturdaypaper.com.au/news/health/2020/04/25/aboriginal-community-healths-success-with-covid-19/15877368009740

Melbourne Law School. *Uluru Statement from the Heart: Information Booklet*. University of Melbourne. law.unimelb.edu.au/__data/assets/pdf_file/0010/2764738/Uluru-Statement-from-the-Heart-Information-Booklet.pdf

Parliament of Australia. *The Australian Constitution*. aph.gov.au/about_parliament/senate/powers_practice_n_procedures/constitution

Pearson, Noel. *A Rightful Place: Race, Recognition and a More Complete Commonwealth.* Black Inc., Australia. 2014.

Phillips, Sandra. 'A Rightful Path: Educating for Change and Achievement'. *Griffith Review 60: First Things First.* 2018. griffithreview.com/articles/rightful-path-education-change-achievement

Uluru Statement from the Heart. 2017. ulurustatement.org

United Nations. *United Nations Declaration on the Rights of Indigenous Peoples.* 2007. un.org/development/desa/indigenouspeoples/declaration-on-the-rights-of-indigenous-peoples.html

Walter, Maggie. 'The Voice of Indigenous Data: Beyond the Markers of Disadvantage', *Griffith Review 60: First Things First.* 2018. griffithreview.com/articles/voice-indigenous-data-beyond-disadvantage

Whittaker, Alison. 'First Nations People Have Faced Moments Like This Before. We Can Learn from the Poems that Sprang from Them'. *Guardian.* 24 April 2020. theguardian.com/books/2020/apr/24/first-nations-people-have-faced-moments-like-this-before-we-can-learn-from-the-poems-that-sprung-from-them

4. EDUCATION AND HEALTH

Babones, Salvatore. 'The China Student Boom and the Risks It Poses to Australian Universities'. Centre for Independent Studies. Analysis Paper 5. August 2019. cis.org.au/app/uploads/2019/08/ap5.pdf

Brett, Judith. *The Coal Curse: Resources, Climate and Australia's Future.* Black Inc., Australia. 2020

Collini, Stefan. *Speaking of Universities.* 2017

Commonwealth of Australia, Department of Health. COVID-19 Cases in Aged Care Services—Residential Care. 2020. health.gov.au/resources/covid-19-cases-in-aged-care-services-residential-care

Commonwealth of Australia, Department of Health. COVID-19 Temporary MBS Telehealth Services: Fact Sheet. 2020. mbsonline.gov.au/internet/mbsonline/publishing.nsf/Content/0C514FB8C9FBBEC7CA25852E00223AFE/$File/Factsheet-COVID-19-Bulk-billed-MBS%20telehealth-Services-Overarching-17.09.2020.pdf

Commonwealth of Australia, Royal Commission into Aged Care Quality and Safety. 'Aged Care and COVID-19: A Special Report'. September 2020. agedcare.royalcommission.gov.au/sites/default/files/2020-10/aged-care-and-covid-19-a-special-report.pdf

Davey, Melissa. '"Ants Crawling from Wounds": Horrifying Scenes at Coronavirus-Hit Aged Care Home in Melbourne'. *Guardian*. 14 August 2020. theguardian.com/australia-news/2020/aug/14/ants-crawling-from-wound-horrifying-scenes-at-coronavirus-hit-aged-care-home-in-melbourne

Denniss, Richard. 'The Spread of Coronavirus in Australia Is Not the Fault of Individuals but a Result of Neoliberalism'. *Guardian*. 20 August 2020. theguardian.com/commentisfree/2020/aug/20/the-spread-of-coronavirus-is-not-the-fault-of-individuals-but-a-result-of-neoliberalism

Eagar, Kathy. 'The (Failing) Aged Care System We Have in 2020 Operates Exactly as It Was Designed To'. *Pearls and Irritations*. 17 August 2020. johnmenadue.com/kathy-eagar-part-1-the-aged-care-system-we-have-in-2020-is-not-a-system-that-is-failing

Forsyth, Hannah. 'Disinterested Scholars or Interested Parties? The Public's Investment in Self-interested Universities'. In Thornton, M. (ed). *Through a Glass Darkly: The Social Sciences Look at the Neoliberal University*. ANU Press, Australia. 2014.

Kenway, Jane et al. 'Seeking the Necessary "Resources of Hope" in the Neoliberal University'. In Thornton, M. (ed.). *Through a Glass Darkly: The Social Sciences Look at the Neoliberal University*. ANU Press, Australia. 2014.

Muller, Jerry. *The Tyranny of Metrics*. Princeton University Press, United States. 2018.

Sydney Local Health District. 'Sydney Local Health District Opens the First Virtual Hospital in New South Wales'. February 2020. slhd.nsw.gov.au/sydneyconnect/story-2020-RPA-Virtua-Hospital.html

United Nations. *Universal Declaration of Human Rights*. 1948. un.org/en/universal-declaration-human-rights

UN News. 'Put Women and Girls at Centre of COVID-19 Recovery: UN Secretary-General'. 9 April 2020. news.un.org/en/story/2020/04/1061452

Wiesel, Ilan. 'Paternalism, Public Housing and COVID-19'. *Pursuit*, University of Melbourne. 27 July 2020. findanexpert.unimelb.edu.au/news/12773-paternalism--public-housing-and-covid-19

Withers, Glenn. 'The State of the Universities'. In Thornton, M. (ed.). *Through a Glass Darkly: The Social Sciences Look at the Neoliberal University*. ANU Press, Australia. 2014.

5. CLIMATE CHANGE AND INDUSTRY

Beyond Zero Emissions. *The Million Jobs Plan: A Unique Opportunity to Demonstrate the Growth and Employment Potential of Investing in a Low-Carbon Economy.* 2020. bze.org.au/wp-content/uploads/BZE-The-Million-Jobs-Plan-Full-Report-2020.pdf

Brett, Judith. *The Coal Curse: Resources, Climate and Australia's Future.* Black Inc., Australia. 2020

Denniss, Richard. *Dead Right: How Neoliberalism Ate Itself and What Came Next.* Black Inc., Australia. 2018.

Flannery, Tim. 'World in Motion'. *Griffith Review 52: Imagining the Future.* 2016. griffithreview.com/articles/21938

Garnaut, Ross. *Superpower: Australia's Low-Carbon Opportunity.* La Trobe University Press in conjunction with Black Inc., Australia. 2019.

Greenpeace Australia Pacific. 'Lethal Power: How Coal Is Killing People in Australia'. 25 August 2020. greenpeace.org.au/research/lethal-power-how-coal-is-killing-people-in-australia

Hepburn, Samantha. '4 Reasons Why a Gas-Led Economic Recovery Is a Terrible, Naive Idea'. *Conversation.* 25 August 2020. theconversation.com/4-reasons-why-a-gas-led-economic-recovery-is-a-terrible-na-ve-idea-145009

Holmes à Court, Simon. 'Australia's Aluminium Sector Is on Life Support. It Can and Should Be Saved'. *Guardian.* 31 October 2019. theguardian.com/commentisfree/2019/oct/31/australias-aluminium-sector-is-on-life-support-it-can-and-should-be-saved

Knuas, Christopher. 'PM's Taskforce Backing Gas Expansion Received Advice from Lobbying Firm with Saudi Links'. *Guardian.* 20 September 2020. theguardian.com/australia-news/2020/sep/20/pms-taskforce-backing-gas-expansion-received-advice-from-lobbying-firm-with-saudi-links

Lukacs, Martin. 'Neoliberalism Has Conned Us into Fighting Climate Change as Individuals'. *Guardian.* 18 July 2017. theguardian.com/environment/true-north/2017/jul/17/neoliberalism-has-conned-us-into-fighting-climate-change-as-individuals

Manne, Robert. *Bad News: Murdoch's* Australian *and the Shaping of the Nation.* Black Inc., Australia. 2011.

Manne, Robert. 'How Can Climate Change Denialism Be Explained?'. *Monthly.* 8 December 2011. themonthly.com.au/blog/robert-manne/2011/12/12/1323650771/how-can-climate-change-denialism-be-explained

Masson-Delmotte, V. et al (eds). *Global Warming of 1.5°C: An IPCC Special Report on the Impacts of Global Warming of 1.5°C Above Pre-industrial Levels and Related Global Greenhouse Gas Emission Pathways, in the Context of Strengthening the Global Response to the Threat of Climate Change, Sustainable Development, and Efforts to Eradicate Poverty.* Intergovernmental Panel on Climate Change. 2019. ipcc.ch/sr15

McDuff, Phil. 'Ending Climate Change Requires the End of Capitalism. Have We Got the Stomach for It?'. *Guardian*. 18 March 2019. theguardian.com/commentisfree/2019/mar/18/ending-climate-change-end-capitalism

Morton, Adam. 'UN Climate Talks: Australia Accused of "Cheating" and Thwarting Global Deal'. *Guardian*. 16 December 2019. theguardian.com/environment/2019/dec/16/un-climate-talks-australia-accused-of-cheating-and-thwarting-global-deal

Taylor, Angus. 'We Should Be Proud of Our Climate Change Efforts', *Australian*. 30 December 2019. theaustralian.com.au/commentary/we-should-be-proud-of-our-climate-change-efforts/news-story/0dec56da908b04a1a55c69f1631c1b52

The Greens. Towards a Green New Deal. 2020. greens.org.au/greennewdeal

Statement from the United Nations Secretary-General António Guterres. 'Global Community Must Not Give Up Tackling Climate Crisis, Secretary-General Says, Expressing Disappointment with Results of Twenty-Fifth Conference'. 15 December 2019. un.org/press/en/2019/sgsm19914.doc.htm

United Nations. *United Nations Framework Convention on Climate Change.* 1992. unfccc.int/resource/docs/convkp/conveng.pdf

United Nations. The Paris Agreement in United Nations Framework Convention on Climate Change. 2016. unfccc.int/process-and-meetings/the-paris-agreement/the-paris-agreement

Wood, Tony et al. 'Start with Steel: A Practical Plan to Support Carbon Workers and Cut Emissions'. Grattan Institute Report No. 2020–06. May 2020. grattan.edu.au/wp-content/uploads/2020/05/2020-06-Start-with-steel.pdf

ACKNOWLEDGMENTS

While this book is short—and was written within a short timeframe—there are many people I nevertheless need to thank.

I think it is true that all writers at some point in their careers wish to be approached by their dream publisher to write a book. This happened to me, and I am ever so grateful for the opportunity my editor at Text, Alaina Gougoulis, gave me. Thank you for taking a chance on me. And thank you to my publicist, Jane Watkins, for working your magic.

To the National Geographic Society, for providing me with a grant to report on the coronavirus in Australia, which began the journey of this book. Thank you.

To my editor at the *London Review of Books*, Thomas Jones, who published my first piece on the coronavirus: thank you for your support.

To everyone I interviewed: thank you for being so generous with your time. I hope I have done justice to the issues we talked about. Your dedication to bettering Australia is inspiring.

A massive thanks to Chris Graham, Aimee Volkofsky and Sarah Donnelly for opening your homes to me and for teaching me so much about north-western NSW.

To my dearest friends in Sydney, Brisbane and Melbourne: you know who you are. Thank you for your unwavering love and encouragement. And to T, I am ever so grateful for your enthusiasm and support.

To Katherine Waters, for not only being my guiding light throughout this book project, but for being the best type of friend anyone could imagine. You truly are one of a kind.

To NES artist residency in Skagaströnd, Iceland: thank you for giving me the quiet space and time to finish off this book. To travel during a pandemic to a place of serene beauty was such a privilege. And to the artists who made the residency what it was, thank you. Special thanks to Andolie, Andra and Kerryn.

Last but certainly not least, to my family, my everything. For the past ten years you have not only put up with my chaotic, crazy work life, you have supported it, encouraged it and nourished it. I am so grateful for the time we got to spend together during this pandemic—without a doubt it was the light amid the dark.